# Positive
# Attitude
# Training

# Positive Attitude Training

## How to Be an Unshakable Optimist

Michael S. Broder, Ph.D.

**MEDIA**

Published 2019 by Gildan Media LLC
aka G&D Media.
www.GandDmedia.com

Copyright © 2019 by Michael S. Broder, Ph.D.

First Edition: 2019

Front cover design by David Rheinhardt of Pyrographx

Interior design by Meghan Day Healey of Story Horse, LLC.

Library of Congress Cataloging-in-Publication Data is available upon request

ISBN: 978-1-7225-0170-9

10  9  8  7  6  5  4  3  2  1

# Contents

# Introduction

I've never believed that like eye color, you're either *born* an optimist or a pessimist. Optimism is merely an *attitude*. And it is your attitudes that determine not only how you feel at a given time, but in reality, the quality of practically every part of your life! The best news of all is that your attitudes toward yourself and others, as well as virtually anything and everything in your life, are one hundred percent under your control—once you have the will, the determination, and the strategies to take charge of them.

The will and determination, of course, only you can provide. Thus, I'll assume that by buying this book, you've joined *that* club. Now, for the strategies, you've certainly come to the right place. When I first wrote *Positive Attitude Training* in 1992 as an extremely successful audio program, my intention was to make it an arsenal of timeless tools, clinically proven techniques, and solutions to issues that that we all face in the course our daily lives. The fact that this book has been written 27 years after the concept of Positive Attitude Training was introduced is a testament to the timelessness of the methods you're about to learn.

So think of Positive Attitude Training as your go-to source for overcoming issues caused by emotional states like anxiety, depression, guilt, and anger; not only managing stress but also making it work *for* you; setting and reaching goals; changing and being in control of your habits; maximizing your self-confidence and self-image; letting go of the past; making major life changes; and a whole lot more.

My website, drmichaelbroder.com, contains many single-issue, user-friendly audio programs, which go into further detail on each of these (and many other) issues— and can be downloaded for *free* if you need more help in any areas. Our mission is simply to give you the tools you need to make your life exactly how you want it.

So, welcome to this new phase of your life, in which as an unshakable optimist, self-imposed limitations will soon be a thing of the past. So many new possibilities await!

Michael S. Broder, Ph.D.

# ONE

# Choosing Your Attitudes

For over forty years I've used, as well as trained thousands of mental health professionals to use, the methods I'm going to talk about in this book, which are all clinically proven to help people choose the attitudes by which they lead their lives. The key word here is *choose*, and I will constantly be reminding you that your choices are what empower you to make your life exactly what you want it to be.

Positive Attitude Training is grounded in cognitive-behavioral therapy (CBT) and also uses many of the techniques of rational emotive behavioral therapy (REBT). This is a well-researched, well-tested, and extremely user-friendly approach that you can easily learn. If you make the commitment to use these principles in your daily life, you'll turn your negative thinking and negative emotions around rapidly.

Many of the principles of cognitive-behavioral therapy were developed by two mentors of mine, Dr. Aaron Beck, the originator of CBT, and Dr. Albert Ellis, who created REBT. Both of these pioneers radically changed the landscape of how we view our attitudes, beliefs, and behaviors, as well as our ability to optimize them.

Both CBT and REBT can be applied to any area of your life, and indeed we will touch on practically all of the issues that we encounter in our daily lives. I will present many user-friendly exercises that you can apply to almost any situation. Some of the material will contain things that you've known all along but perhaps never heard articulated, while other ideas may be entirely new.

You may find it helpful to keep a diary to keep track of the insights that come up along the way, or you may find that some of the material raises more questions than answers. If that's the case, the answers will come along, but in the meantime you may want to keep track of the questions so that when the time is right, you can plug them into the appropriate exercise.

Let's begin with the definition of an *attitude*. An attitude is an organized and enduring set of beliefs and feelings toward an object, a person, or a situation. Our attitudes predispose us to behave in certain ways toward something or someone. In other words, our attitudes make our reactions to things predictable.

Attitudes have three components: a *cognitive component*, your beliefs; an *emotional component*, your feelings; and a *behavioral component*, your actions, or what you do about the attitudes you have.

Our attitudes are often developed when we're very young. In many cases, they are quite ingrained in us. They're often taught to us in such a way that we grow up believing that we have no choice. Sometimes our blind acceptance of attitudes causes us to have fear, anger, depression, prejudice, and self-doubts. This can make us quite vulnerable to the negative effects of daily stress.

The good news is that since our attitudes are learned, they can be unlearned, and new ones that we choose can be adopted in the place of the old ones. Some attitudes are unlearned and relearned quite easily, while others require a great deal of repetition. But rarely is an attitude changed in one fell swoop.

Before I get into the particulars of how this is done, let me briefly explain cognitive-behavioral theory. It operates on a simple premise: that our belief about a given event— that is, what is internal to us—is the real cause of our emotional consequences or how we feel about the event, rather than the event itself being the cause of what we feel. In other words, our emotions, for the most part, are caused internally, not externally.

For example, suppose you began to experience depression shortly after losing your job. Normally, you would attribute that depression to the job loss, which of course is an external event. Cognitive-behavioral theory, however, would show you that it was not the job loss that caused your depression, but your *belief* about that job loss. Thus you could be telling yourself, "I'm incompetent. My family and I will starve. Now I will have to carry the stigma of being unemployed," or "There's nothing to look forward to."

By seeing that the depression you're feeling is attributable mainly to your beliefs about the job loss—beliefs which can be challenged and changed—you will see that your depression can become resolved regardless of whether or not you find a job.

We call this the *elegant solution,* where the problem is resolved on an internal or emotional level. The practical or empirical solution, of course, would be for you to find another job, and the behavioral part of this approach will help you to do that as well. But with the elegant solution, lessening the depression does not depend on those outside forces, such as when and whether you get a job, which may be beyond your control.

Moreover, getting another job would only solve the problem temporarily, unless you are fortunate enough to never again lose a job. Thus the elegant solution can also resolve the problem on a permanent basis.

Throughout this book, you will learn just how to do this with all the issues presented, and with practice, this approach will quickly effect permanent attitude change. Once you've learned this, the ability to have a positive attitude is yours forever. Think about the choices you want to make in your life and what it is that holds you back. Act as though there are no acceptable excuses, because in life, that's truly your reality.

Ultimately you are responsible for what you do. That's not just a cliché. It's a fact. You can blame others or yourself all you want, but the only thing that will really make a difference is to make a choice and to stand behind your choices.

If you've been treating your life as though it's been only a dress rehearsal, now is the time to realize that the show's begun. The main attraction is happening right now, and it can be a very good one, with rave reviews, or it can be a flop. What makes the difference is what you have chosen.

In fact the argument can be made that practically everything you have in your life is a result of some choice you've made, either consciously or unconsciously. Sometimes you've thought things through; other times, you may have simply gone with your feelings. Neither course alone is always the one that works best. Children act solely on their feelings practically all the time, and we try to teach them to think things through. On the other hand, as adults, we often lose the spontaneity we had as kids and need to reconnect with our feelings.

Some choices may have come to you easily, while others may have been very difficult. Some have even been made unconsciously. This is all part of the human condition. The problem comes when, instead of accepting reality as it is, you tell yourself that it should be another way.

Think for a moment about how nice life could be if there were no *shoulds*—if we didn't tell ourselves that life *should* have no issues, that other people *should* be the way we want them to be rather than the way they are, that we *should* do better than our best, or that our life in the world *should* be easy. When you adopt attitudes that eliminate those *shoulds*, far fewer things in life will disturb you.

Behind practically every negative attitude there's a *should* statement that we make, either consciously or unconsciously, that leads to a disturbing emotion. For example, the last time you were angry, weren't you telling yourself that someone *should* have treated you better or that your expectations *should* have been better met? The last time you were down on yourself, perhaps because things didn't go the way you wanted them to, weren't you telling yourself that you should have done better, even though chances are that you did the best you could at that time?

See if you can identify with some of these nine traps or thinking errors, which we all make from time to time and account for most of our negative feelings.

- The first one is demanding certainty. That is putting off important decisions or actions because you believe that it is imprudent to act unless you are certain of a positive outcome. Certainty is a myth—perhaps one of the most widely perpetuated ones, but a myth nonetheless.

- Second is defining something as too hard or impossible when, in fact, it is merely difficult. By doing that, you're likely to procrastinate, and worse yet, to put yourself down for it afterwards.

- Third is telling yourself that life is awful, terrible, and catastrophic when things don't go the way you want them to. In fact, 99 percent of your life could be exactly as you want it to be, but that 1 percent that isn't going well can, if you let it, serve to negate all the good stuff.

- Fourth, do you label yourself in a globally negative way merely because you made a mistake or failed in a task? Rather than recognizing that it's the behavior that's negative, do you put yourself down or define yourself as incompetent? If that's the case, then it's quite possible that you spend a great deal of your time struggling with self-acceptance.

- Fifth, maybe you tend to rate others in totally negative terms simply because they did not come through for you the way you wanted or expected them to. If so, it's quite possible you could be spending a lot of your time being consumed with anger.

- Sixth, do you hold yourself to impossible standards? If so, it's possible that you spend a lot of your time being anxious and down on yourself.

- Seventh, if you require that other people give you love and approval as a prerequisite for accepting yourself, then you could be spending an excessive amount of time pleasing others to the exclusion of what really works for you.

- Eighth, do you think in black-and-white terms, that is, all or nothing? When something is short of perfect, do you see it as a total failure? If so, you may be spending a lot of your time being stressed, and others may experience you as being somewhere between difficult and impossible to please.

- Ninth and finally, you could be believing that because you had a certain type of childhood or certain life experiences, happiness or other types of achievement in life are now impossible. If so, you could be turning that into a self-fulfilling prophecy.

All of these beliefs cause self-defeating attitudes. To the extent that you have them, you have chosen them, perhaps unconsciously, but now is the time to turn that all around.

The theologian Reinhold Niebuhr said, "Grant me the serenity to accept the things that I cannot change, the courage to change the things I can, and the wisdom to know the difference." In what he famously called The Serenity Prayer, he was talking about knowing the difference between the practical or empirical and the emotional or elegant solution to a problem. Those things that disturb you, but which you cannot change, need to be accepted; otherwise the result is likely to be emotional pain and upset. The things that can be changed are what warrant your greatest efforts and focus. This is about doing what it takes to enable you to take charge of your life, which is your deepest duty to yourself.

Before we talk about change, let me give you an illustration of how individualized our beliefs about one external event can be. When I was a freshman in college, I worked at a gas station. The date was November 22, 1963. It was early that Friday afternoon when a woman came into the station and told us that President Kennedy had been shot. Several of us were standing around, and we looked at this woman in disbelief. A minute or so later, someone else came in and told us the same thing.

Immediately, we turned on the radio, and very shortly that gas station became an impromptu community room. Within a few minutes, there were perhaps twenty or thirty people standing around listening to the news. When it was announced that the president had died, most of us were stunned and saddened. One woman broke into hysterics and ran out of the station, even leaving her car behind. Someone else knocked over a countertop display in rage. One man expressed the hope that perhaps the new president would go into Vietnam and do what had to be done. He was actually happy about the news. Another person expressed a view that Kennedy had led a good life, and he was older than a relative of his who had died recently—since people seemed to have taken that with a grain a salt, what was the big deal about this?

What stayed with me the most about that afternoon was how so many different emotional reactions came out of one singular event. Depending on what you believed about Kennedy, death, and the assassination of a president, you all seemed to develop your own custom-made emotional reactions.

This is the way emotions are formed—through beliefs. Changing an attitude involves choosing a new belief. This is sometimes called an *affirmation*. An affirmation is a new belief that you can choose to replace a self-defeating belief that was behind a negative attitude—one that you may have acquired automatically. When you have attitudes about life or about yourself that are harmful and get in the way of your happiness, then what you need is a new affirmation.

Let's go back to the example of losing your job through no fault of your own, causing you economic hardship. That situation in and of itself can be difficult enough, but when you complicate it by blaming yourself—even though you know the situation was out of your control and was not your choice—your attitude can make the impact many times worse. As you can see, blaming yourself certainly won't help solve the problem.

One step toward resolving this problem is to identify the affirmation that will help you to stop blaming yourself.

It might be something like, "True, these are difficult times, but blaming myself will only make them more painful."

An affirmation can be what you know to be true, but don't yet believe, or what you know in your head but not in your heart, that is, what you know intellectually but not emotionally.

"I know it intellectually, but"—how often have I heard that! It means that you know it sometimes, or as it applies to other people. For example, you know that someone who is laid off as a result of an economic situation should not be blamed or put down, but do you believe it? You know that to err is human, but do you give yourself permission to make mistakes? If not, this is called *perfectionism*, and it can cause a lot of self-criticism, self-doubting, and stress.

I'm going to teach you how to tell your gut what your head already knows. Sometimes that involves knowing the difference between insight and hindsight. Many confuse these two seemingly similar concepts. Insight is a healthy and positive process that takes place when you have an experience from which you are able to learn. Hindsight, on the other hand, is where you look back on a situation that has already occurred and tell yourself, "If I had known then what I know now, I would have done it differently."

Wouldn't we all? We all know that hindsight is 20/20, but you may not realize how unhealthy it really is, especially if you put yourself down for not having acted on information that couldn't possibly have been at your disposal. For example, in hindsight, would Kennedy have gone to Dallas that day? Hindsight is akin to reading the daily paper with yesterday's winning lottery number and condemning yourself for not having chosen it. Insight, on the other hand, increases self-acceptance, and that can make practically any problem ultimately a no-lose situation. For instance, the insight gained from Kennedy's assassination was to provide future presidents with far better security.

So we'll concentrate on creating new ways for you to access your insight, and remember: insight is using a learning experience to look at something in a new and different way. Insight will change practically any problem into a no-lose situation, simply by showing you that you not only can stand the problem but can learn from it as well. But insight is worthless unless you use it. Just having an insight in your head isn't enough, while putting it to work for you will change your life.

We'll also look at *simple* versus *easy*. Many people confuse the two concepts. A lot of the approaches that I talk about in changing an attitude sound very simple. Indeed they are simple, but they're not necessarily easy to enact.

If you asked me how to drive from one coast to another, I could say, "Get on such-and-such a highway and stay on it for 3,000 miles, and it'll get you there. Simple, isn't it?" But making the drive, as anyone who's ever done it will tell you, is far from easy. Often we think of our inability to change situations in those terms. Repetition, as well as attacking your resistance to change, will make the crucial difference.

Here are a few other principles that I would like you to keep in mind as we work on designing new attitudes together.

You have the power to be or do practically anything you want. You can have practically anything you want in life, but you probably can't have *everything* you want. A limitation is an inability to make certain specific changes, either in your life or the world, that are important for you to make. Accepting your limitations is an important part of self-acceptance, but it is one of the most difficult things for most of us to do. We know how intellectually, but have a lot of trouble learning it on a gut level.

Are you able to accept your own limitations? Remember, having it all is a myth. We achieve peace of mind when we're not worrying about something that's taken place in the past, going over events that have ended, or telling ourselves that we or someone else should have done or said something differently.

You know how you can feel when you're focused on the present moment and not concerned with what has already happened or with what's going to happen in the future. And that future can be five minutes from now, tomorrow, next week, or next year. Letting go of these obsessions with the past and the future can help you achieve a peaceful and mindful frame of mind.

Peace of mind can also be defined as those moments that are free of shoulds. Sometimes feeling dissatisfied is healthy, because it forces you to take something to the next level. On the other hand, it could mean that you've set standards so high that nothing satisfies you. So a worthwhile goal may sometimes be to consider your lack of satisfaction a friend rather than an enemy.

Many books have been written about the meaning of life, but in its simplest form, the meaning of your life is simply what meaning you give it, either consciously, that is, deliberately, or unconsciously, sometimes even by default. If you feel that your life is lacking meaning, then it's quite possible that there's nothing you feel truly committed to. So the first step is to look at what you *are* genuinely committed to. That is where you will find your meaning.

If you see someone who you think has a better life than you, sure, you can attribute it to luck, the person they're married to, the fact that they inherited money, or something else, but remember that all the things that occur outside the parameters of your free will are subject to change with the wind. Only what you have inside of you is yours forever.

## Strategies to Get started on Positive Attitude Change

Here are a few exercises you may try to get started on your road toward positive attitude change.

- Ask yourself, if you could have whatever you wanted in life, what would it be? What would you like your life to be? Answer this question as creatively as you can. Make a list as long as necessary of all those things you would like.

- Make a list of all the things that stand in your way of getting each item on your list. We'll be working both on these goals and on your obstacles throughout this book, but, for now, just let your imagination run wild.

- Keep a log of thoughts that come to you when you become upset. Write down what you're thinking each time you experience a negative emotion, such as when you feel sad, angry, or nervous. No one else has to see your log, but you'll find that this information will come in handy for identifying some of your main negative thoughts, attitudes, and triggers.

- Make a list of those things that you know in your head that you wish your gut knew, things that you would like your head to tell your gut. It may help to put them on 3" x 5" cards or in your smartphone and remind yourself to look at them several times a day. Attitudes and beliefs are learned, and this is an important step in deliberately using your inner wisdom to help you to do just that.

- Each time you get angry or upset, ask yourself, "Is the situation a minor inconvenience, a major inconvenience, or is it really a catastrophe?" Rarely, if ever, will the latter ring true. Then ask the next question. "Is there something I need to accept, change, or understand about this upset?" If there's something that you need to accept, see if you can come up with an elegant or emotional solution, and put it in the form of an affirmation. If there's something that needs to be changed, think about what it is that you're going to do differently. If there's something you need to understand, ask yourself, "What is the insight here"?

Think of building positive attitudes the same way you would think of building up your body. You can get yourself into terrific shape, but if you let your body go, it'll go right back to the way it was. The same is true about adopting positive attitudes. Life circumstances will challenge you and will often undermine your progress, but it's up to you to make a vigorous and ongoing commitment to staying in optimal mental shape.

Never forget how complex we are. After all, if the brain were so simple that we had the capacity to fully understand it, then we'd probably be too simpleminded to do much with the knowledge. Most importantly, don't take yourself too seriously. If you can remember that, then you've laid perhaps the most important cornerstone of positive attitude change.

# TWO

# Frustration:
# How Much Can You Stand?

Do you get frustrated easily? If so, do you think frustration is a positive or a negative thing? For most people, the word *frustration* conjures up images of being caught in traffic, being bored with a relationship, trying to achieve something in your career that's out of your reach, or even trying to change someone else's mind.

If you think about it, on some level practically every area of your life where you've made progress or change has come as a result of some degree of frustration. Frustration is usually the thing that alerts us to make changes or to come up with new ideas. For example, the chair I'm sitting on was probably originally invented by someone who became frustrated with sitting on the floor. Often career advancement is motivated by the frustration of feeling trapped at a lower level.

So if there's something that you're frustrated about, you may want to ask yourself, "Just what is it in my life that needs attention right now?" Then take a look at whatever you've defined as needing change and decide if that change is within your power to effect. If so, then you may know what action to take, or perhaps determining that action can be the next step in your thinking.

You may be thinking that frustration is a negative thing because you confuse it with what we call *low frustration tolerance*, or LFT. When you have something that's frustrating you, instead of constructively looking it in the eye and making the changes that need to be made or working to accept the things that you can't change, you tell yourself that you cannot stand whatever is frustrating you. Then you wind up at an impasse. In other words, you overreact to any kind of discomfort that you face in your life, large or small. That's why we also call low frustration tolerance *discomfort anxiety*. If you think I'm talking about something that's prevalent, you bet I am. Self-defeating addictions such as overeating, smoking, drug and alcohol abuse, and gambling are all to some degree symptoms of low frustration tolerance.

Procrastination is definitely a form of low frustration tolerance. Avoiding certain pleasures that also have hassles or discomfort attached to them, such as dating or social-izing when you're feeling isolated, is an expression of LFT as well. So is shyness: instead of conquering it by exposing yourself to situations that may make you feel a little uncomfortable, you avoid them completely, rather than tolerating the frustration that is inevitability part of the discomfort.

Perhaps you pick easy goals rather than ones that would be more challenging, interesting, or enjoyable, or you stay at a lower-level job rather than looking for advancement, even though working harder toward a more rewarding goal would benefit you in the long run. Maybe you give up on projects that are important to you as soon as they get a little tedious.

All these are symptoms of low frustration tolerance. Other examples of LFT include boredom, getting involved with love or sex partners who may be exciting at first but who will not be there for you in the long run, and the opposite—leaving potentially good relationships or jobs because they include some hassle or inconvenience that you would rather avoid than confront. Some people even have no frustration tolerance. Whenever anything is frustrating, they run away, engage in some other kind of blatant avoidance, or strike like a cornered rat.

So whenever you're feeling anxious or angry, it's important for you to look at what's frustrating you and then face it head-on by recognizing your attitude toward it. That's the first step toward turning frustration, an inevitability in life, into a friend rather than an enemy.

Suppose you have an important project to finish. Your children are making an inordinate amount of noise, and you find yourself reacting very angrily toward them. Is it the noise that's making you angry, or is it the fact that you're not tolerating the inevitable frustration that comes when you're trying to concentrate and someone is making noise?

If you'd just kept it on the level of frustration, you'd probably find another place to work, make some other arrangements for your children, or solve the problem in another way, so that everyone could have a little piece of what they need. But when low frustration tolerance kicks in and you tell yourself, "I can't stand this noise anymore," or "These children are ruining my life by annoying me when I have something so important to do," that frustration takes on a life of its own. It makes the situation seem like a horror rather than the mere inconvenience that it really is.

Suppose that while balancing your checkbook, you were to find out that you made a mistake, and you had $1,000 less in the bank than you thought. At first, you think that it's your fault you made an error, and you become very angry at yourself. Is it that perceived loss of $1,000 that made you angry, or is it the fact that you're telling yourself, "How stupid can I be for making a mistake like that?"

Suppose you found out it was your spouse who made the error. Would you then become angry because of the error, or would your anger come more from telling yourself, "I cannot stand it when people make stupid errors"? It's that very belief that you cannot stand it that is the culprit here.

Think about it. Isn't that statement "I can't stand it" inaccurate? I would be hard-pressed to name anything about which I have said "I can't stand it" that I wasn't in fact standing. Instead what I meant was, "I don't like it," and that is merely a call for action. By saying, "I don't like it," you're recognizing a problem that needs to be addressed, whereas saying, "I can't stand it," will trigger the painful emotions of anger, anxiety, and depression.

If you are acting from your low frustration tolerance, chances are you're choosing a short-term goal over a long-term goal. Examples include procrastination: by putting something off at this moment, you'll have to face the consequences later on. Addictions such as overeating, smoking, and drug and alcohol abuse give you immediate short-term benefit, but as you know, they can do you considerable harm in the long run.

This brings us to another major belief behind the LFT attitude—a tendency to label things that are merely difficult as too hard.

Confusing *hard* and *too hard* may sound like nitpicking, but the distinction could spell the difference between success and failure in your life. Let me tell you what I mean.

Most things that are worthwhile have some level of difficulty attached to them. Accomplishing practically anything that's difficult or hard will have some built-in frustration along the way, but the rewards will take some time to reap. *Too hard*, however, implies *impossible*. Once you label something as too hard, it becomes something that you will probably stop seriously attempting. I have seen students sabotage their long-term goals by refusing to finish their college education because they label the endeavor as too hard, which it isn't, rather than difficult, which it is.

Try this simple exercise: Think of something that you have constantly put off because you labeled it as being too hard. It could be something like painting your house or taking the first step toward a career change.

Next, think of a reward that you really would like to have. It could be anything, even a great car or a million dollars or some form of fame. Now answer this: if you could be guaranteed that reward, as far-fetched as it may be, could you and would you complete that task on time and to your satisfaction?

If you have answered yes, then you've proved that your definition of this task as too hard has been an illusion that you can do without. If you can hold on to that concept when you're up against a challenge, you'll be able to accomplish almost anything you set out to do without being sabotaged by low frustration tolerance.

## Strategies to Conquer Your LFT

Here are some other exercises you can do to conquer your LFT. Remember: this is really discomfort anxiety. Challenge that erroneous belief that you can't stand discomfort.

- Make a list of those things that can typically trigger your being uncomfortable. On your list include all of the things you tell yourself you cannot stand.

- Come up with alternative attitudes. For example, if there's a coworker that you thoroughly disrespect, try to reframe dealing with that person as a challenge rather than as an agony or a trap from which there's no way out. If it's a project that triggers your low frustration tolerance, see it as an adventure or a contest to finish rather than as an ongoing source of torture.

- Make a list of the advantages of disciplining yourself in this manner. Sure, change is hard, but the changes we're talking about here are in your own best interest to make. See how many things in your life there are to which you can apply this principle.

- Imagine someone you care about being bothered by the thing that is triggering your low frustration tolerance. What would you tell that person? Chances are, you would give him or her lots of support in developing an attitude that would produce comfort rather than tension and stress. Or deliberately put yourself in a situation that you know you will experience as frustrating, just to prove to yourself that you really can stand it.

For example, each holiday season, clients who have recently ended love relationships tell me that being alone for the holidays is going to be a horror. Many frantically make plans so that they won't have to spend their time alone. They believe this time should only be spent with friends and loved ones, just as it may have been during that best holiday season of their lives.

Instead, I urge them to deliberately and defiantly spend the worst day they can imagine, such as Christmas Eve or Christmas Day or New Year's Eve, alone, with no contact with the outside world. In the process, they are forced to be their only resource at a time when they believe that they need others to survive it. The people who do this never again fear being alone during the holidays.

If you try this, you'll see what I mean. Because you'll have faced the enemy head-on and proven to yourself that you can stand it. That doesn't necessarily mean that you'll like it, but no longer will it pose a threat to you. Whenever you expose yourself to the things that make you most uncomfortable, you build emotional muscle.

Many have an extremely difficult time waiting in lines. They get frustrated, stressed out, and impatient about this ordeal. I often recommend that they deliberately find some long lines to wait in, just to prove to themselves that they can stand the very thing they say they can't.

This next exercise is an imagery exercise.

• Close your eyes and imagine yourself being thrust into a very uncomfortable situation that would trigger your low frustration tolerance. Really imagine being in that situation—being around the person you don't like, or working on a tedious task that you have told yourself is too hard. Make it one that really puts you in touch with your LFT. Let yourself strongly feel the feelings and emotions that come when you challenge yourself to the max in this manner.

While doing this, be aware of all the emotions your image conjures up. Now begin to give yourself some new affirmations, ones that will go along with a new positive attitude, such as, "I can get along without the immediate gratification that I tell myself I need, even though it would be nice to have everything I want. This is a hassle, but not the horror that I've made it out to be. I do have the power to get through this without causing myself upset."

When giving yourself these new affirmations, see how differently you feel merely by changing the belief about something that has caused you frustration or discomfort. That is a new positive attitude that's yours to keep. When you've accomplished this, give yourself a reward.

Some people find it useful to reward themselves for making these changes, or to punish themselves in some way for slipping backward. For example, think of something that you enjoy, some kind of special treat, something that you can give yourself as a reward for adopting a new attitude. By the same token, think of something that you dislike, a chore or something that you would rather not be exposed to. We call these *negative contingencies*. As we will see later on when we talk about habits, negative contingencies are very effective in keeping you on track.

Eventually, these new positive attitudes and their affirmations become second nature, just as the old, negative attitudes were, but in the meantime, you may have to exert some special and consistent effort to keep this new attitude in the forefront so that you don't slip backward. Try to associate, if possible, with people who are more disciplined. See if they can share a secret or two with you about how they stay on track. Anytime you develop a new and chosen attitude that works for you, resolve to never let anyone pull you backward!

# THREE

# Managing Anger 101

Anger, hostility, rage, fury, cynicism, and aggression are all, to one degree or another, symptoms of low frustration tolerance. Just about all anger is grounded in the idea that someone or something did not meet your expectations.

Think about the last time you were angry. Weren't you telling yourself that the person who was the object of your anger should have treated you better? Or you may have been thinking, "I can't stand the way you're acting toward me," or "You are a terrible person for treating me this way," or "The world is not fair and just," or "Bad things should only happen to bad people, and good things should happen to good people." You get the idea.

There go those shoulds again. In reality, we are powerless to control another person, but, boy, do we try. While many situations are under our control, there are also many that aren't, and those things that get us the angriest are usually those that are not within our control. The good news, however, is that because we now know that our attitudes are within our power to change, we can free ourselves from this potentially lethal emotion.

No one could dispute the fact that there are some legitimate sources of anger. They could include neglect and abuse, unworkable relationships, loss, injustice, unfair treatment, day-to-day hassles, or disruptions in our lives that are out of our sphere of influence.

Usually when we feel angry, we feel self-righteous, and this gives us the illusion that we have the right to blame others for our emotions, but anger has many disadvantages. They include ill effects on your health: studies have shown that anger and cynicism are correlated to premature coronaries.

Anger is emotionally painful. If you want to get even with someone in a malicious way, isn't there usually a tendency to cause them to get angry? Although their anger may be directed at you, you know that it's causing them more pain than it's causing you. Think of that from your own standpoint when you get angry. Is the person you're getting angry at the one who is suffering, or is it you who are suffering? The answer is obvious.

Anger can also be a signal that something needs to be addressed with someone in your life. Perhaps an issue needs to be talked over or resolved. In that case, look upon your angry feeling as a healthy symptom and settle the problem. Sometimes anger sidetracks our efforts to change, because trying to get others to do things our way makes us compulsive and obsessed with revenge, which we know all too well is usually futile.

Anger is often the antecedent to violent behavior and to doing things that are ultimately self-defeating, such as leaving a good job or a relationship, when we would have probably acted differently if we had resolved our anger and been more able to make a rational choice.

Of course, acting angrily sometimes gets things done. I recently acted that way when someone lit up in the no-smoking section of a restaurant. When I asked him nicely to put the cigarette out, he refused. I acted angrily and aggressively by raising my voice, and he finally did. Honestly, I didn't feel nearly as angry as I acted, but in this case, my demeanor got the job done.

There's a distinction here: I was able to do this without burning the stomach acid that I would have if I were truly feeling angry. So assertion should not be confused with anger.

Many couples have told me that their best sex comes right after they've made up following an argument. Anger triggers passion of the negative variety, and sometimes when it's resolved, there's a feeling of release which brings on a positive passion. But these couples are usually consulting me to help them to stop the anger that causes their fighting in the first place. Ironically, many of them don't see the connection.

There are two different schools of thought regarding how anger is best dealt with. Some say it's better to express it. Let it all hang out. Get release. Get relief, and let those you're angry with really know what you're feeling. Others say it's better to keep it in or suppress it. Don't let anyone else know what you're feeling. In other words, deny it to others or even to yourself.

I believe that it's in your best interest to adopt the attitudes that will allow you to bypass this destructive emotion. But if you do get angry, learn to conquer it by using many of the same techniques we discussed for overcoming low frustration tolerance.

## Strategies to Resolve Your Anger

The following attitudes will go a long way in helping you to resolve your anger. In reality, no one can really hurt you emotionally unless you allow it. So the next time you get angry, instead of blaming the anger on the other person, you can attribute that other person's behavior to him or her, but attribute your anger to your own attitude.

People will treat you the way they choose to treat you. Sometimes this will be positive and pleasant, and other times it will not, so the first step in coming to grips with anger is to rid yourself of the illusion that you can control other people, the world, or events in it.

- Distinguish between healthy and unhealthy cynicism. The danger comes when you're unable to draw this line. Healthy cynicism is really skepticism, but the feeling that makes you constantly tense, where you find yourself suspicious and unaffected by new ideas, is the kind of cynicism most associated with anger.

- Ask yourself why others should treat you the way you want them to. Where did you get that notion the world is fair and just anyway? Just pick up any newspaper, and it's apparent that the world is a profoundly unjust place. So when you begin to feel angry, if you react by challenging your own belief system, you'll adopt attitudes that will make you much less vulnerable to external sources.

- Try this exercise. Think of something that would ordinarily get you angry—perhaps being treated rudely, being the object of some insensitive remark, or being cut off in traffic. Now really allow that feeling of anger to escalate so that you experience the tension in your body and you begin to feel righteous and justified; maybe you will even feel yourself shaking slightly.

  When you get to that point, ask yourself, "What alternative attitude can I have at this moment?" Your affirmations may include "The world is going to treat me the way they're going to treat me, and I can't control other people's behavior," or "Why should I put myself through these painful emotions in addition to having to deal with what is upsetting me?"

Whatever it is, see if you can develop a new affirmation that works for you and notice how differently you feel when you can plug it into this situation you've imagined.

Next, practice this with something real in your life whenever you begin to get angry, and you will find that you will begin to develop an immunity to this most harmful emotion, with practice, very quickly. The second that you accept the fact that life is difficult, you will immediately release yourself from the illusion that it should be easy. As you read on, you'll see how these principles apply to other emotions as well.

# FOUR

# Overcoming Depression

You've seen how our own attitudes are what create the painful feeling of anger in us. The same is true with other feelings as well.

First, let's look at depression. And before we begin, let me stipulate that I am referring to the type of depression that's *nonmedical*. Depression should always be evaluated by a mental health professional, since when it is medical in nature it may not respond to the type of strategies I present in this chapter, which speaks to reactive depression. This is the type of depression that's triggered by external events and/or your view of them as well as your own self-perception.

It's been said that anger and depression are bookends, that is, different expressions of the same emotion. Anger is expressed differently, of course, because its focus is generally outward when things aren't going right or when someone doesn't treat you well. With anger, you focus the blame outward, toward the other person or thing, or the world in general. Depression, on the other hand, is expressed inwardly. When you're depressed, you often down yourself by saying, "I should have done better than I did," or "I must succeed in order to be worthwhile."

Anger is an overreaction to frustration, annoyance, or inconvenience caused by something outside of yourself. Depression is generally an overreaction to sadness, grief, regret, or disappointment, and it is accompanied by a self-demand that your performance in a certain area of your life far exceed what it has been. Sadness may be appropriate for people who have experienced loss, but depression usually concerns your inability to bring the lost person or job, for instance, back. Anger and depression both have one very important thing in common: they are either caused by or greatly enhanced by your own tendency to demand what you do not or cannot have, either from yourself or from others.

Depression is often a feeling of hopelessness—feeling stuck in a situation that you tell yourself you would not choose and cannot change. Doesn't this sound like a trap? Well, it certainly is quite common. In fact, all of us at one time or another, to one degree or another, have experienced it.

Depression is often connected with isolation. Many people who are in transition, such as those who are getting out of a relationship, feel depressed and hopeless while going through the grieving process. Perhaps you have built walls to prevent others from getting close to you as a result of being depressed. If that's the case, the good news is that you can tear those walls down.

Depression can manifest itself in many ways. While there are frequently complaints of sadness, a low mood, or melancholia, these are not inevitable. For some people, depression is merely a loss of energy, motivation, or drive, or an inability to derive pleasure from those things that are normally satisfying. Fatigue, loneliness, the inability to relax, poor concentration, difficulties with work, disturbances of appetite, and the loss of sexual desire are frequently signs of depression. Sleep disturbances are particularly common.

For some people, the symptoms of depression are merely physical. Headaches and related symptoms may be masking an underlying depression, and indeed the causes can be either physical or psychological. Internally caused depression is called *endogenous depression*, and it is primarily due to a chemical imbalance. As previously noted, endogenous depression generally does not respond solely to psychotherapy or to changing your attitude; it needs to be evaluated and treated medically, with antidepressants. This cannot be overstated! Once the chemical balance is restored, the antidepressants can often be discontinued. The success rate for treating endogenous depression is quite high, and I urge you to get an immediate evaluation if you think this might be the case for you.

However, the kind of depression that I'm going to emphasize here is depression that is reactive, or related to life events. That is, you're reacting or overreacting to something that's occurred outside of you, or you're reacting to your own thinking about yourself or external events. Just as anger has been correlated to ulcers and heart disease, depression has been correlated to cancer as well as to many other illnesses.

Another reason it's appropriate to talk about anger and depression together is that depression is often anger turned inward. This can both result in and be a result of a great deal of self-downing. The first step in changing your attitudes that underlie depression is to identify the demands that you're making on yourself that you cannot possibly fulfill.

Are you down on yourself because you think you should have accomplished more? Are you blaming yourself over a loss, either a recent one or one that took place long ago? Have you somehow found yourself becoming isolated, with few people or no one to rely on for support? Sometimes you simply need to let go of a disappointment and/or stop defining yourself as incompetent. This attitude turns your depression into a vicious circle.

Many people find that when they're depressed, they reach out to others for support. But well-meaning friends and relatives tend to give them that lethal thing we call *sympathy* instead of much-needed empathy. Except during the most acute stages of grieving, sympathy usually does more harm than good, because when people sympathize, they can be unwittingly telling you that it's right for you to be defining the situation as awful. This can add fuel to the fire.

Empathy, on the other hand, is where the other person will help you to reason the situation out and talk it through without negating your feelings. This kind of empathy can also be extremely important with anger. Reasoning the situation out and expressing your emotions in a safe way is a good way to get relief.

Remember, it's depression that makes sadness, grief, regret, and disappointment last, because depression has a much more lasting quality about it than do other moods. In fact it's worth mentioning that moods are transient. Think about the last time you felt intense joy. Although you would have loved it to, it certainly didn't last. Well, the same is true with negative emotions. If you let them go—something we'll discuss a little later on—they will.

## Strategies to Defeat Depression

Another way to get relief from depression includes getting exercise. The opposite of depression is expression. Often your depression makes you feel unmotivated to do the very things that will help you to break out of it, but at those times, it's essential to push hard against that lack of motivation. Your attitude here can make or break you.

If possible, try to see some humor in the situation that you're depressed about. If you can do that, then you're 90 percent of the way there. There's a light aspect of practically any situation, no matter how dire it is. Remember, this is done in the privacy of your own mind. Don't burden yourself with how others would feel about your effort to look for humor.

Do something nice for yourself. Maybe treat yourself to something you enjoy, a positive diversion, whatever turns you on, whether that means going shopping or listening to some of your favorite music. Some people find relief by accomplishing chores they would rather not do when they're feeling good. As someone recently told me, "When I'm feeling good, that's the time when I want to go fishing, not pay the bills. When I'm feeling down, then I'm not really open to enjoying fun things."

When you're in a rotten mood, reach out to that person who always seems to talk to you when he or she is in a bad mood. See if you can express your feelings with the help of someone who makes the atmosphere safe for you. Understand that you're merely ventilating, and when you ventilate safely, you're just letting out some steam. This can help to break up a negative mood, and again, it's your attitude that will give you permission to do this.

Taking a walk or a ride or just changing your environment for a short period of time can often help. Do something to restore order in your life. Clean up; rearrange some furniture, your office drawers, or your wallet. Sometimes creating order out of chaos is what you need to change a negative mood.

The fact is you know what you enjoy: you know what helps you to lift your mood. Make a list of those things and keep it handy as an emergency checklist. Refer to it whenever you need to.

The most important thing about turning depression around is to give up on demands that you put on yourself but can't possibly live up to. Depression is often a reaction to hindsight. If you catch yourself telling yourself what you should have done, remember, that's not an option, and the faster you give it up, the faster that depression will dissipate.

# FIVE

# Anxiety, Worry, and Guilt

Anxiety has been called fear of the unknown. As we will see, that definition doesn't hold up anymore, because if you think about it, you'll see what's behind your anxiety when you're feeling it.

Before we get to anxiety, let's look at the better-known emotion—anxiety's cousin *fear*. Biologically, man, like most animals, has been equipped with a fear response. That is, when there's an impending danger, we feel the tendency toward fight or flight. When you're feeling fear, usually your instinct is either to run away from or put up a fight against the thing that's frightening you.

Panic is an extreme manifestation of fear, and it can be debilitating. When you panic, often you freeze up and put yourself right in the line of fire of whatever you're fearing. Our instincts toward fear have helped us to survive as a species, but in today's world, rarely does our fear response help us except when we're in imminent physical danger. In fact, there's plenty of evidence that fear and anxiety do more to wreak havoc than anything else.

Anxiety is physiologically identical to fear (and to panic), but the main difference is that fear has a definite object, about which fear is appropriate. Behind appropriate fear, there's an actual danger. Anxiety, on the other hand, does not have a threat behind it that could put you in actual jeopardy. Like most forms of self-doubt, anxiety is perhaps the only disease where the cure is to ignore it and actually do or expose yourself to whatever makes you anxious (within, of course, the limits that you rationally choose for yourself).

What are the designated fears behind that anxiety? Let me name a few here. There's the fear of ridicule or criticism, that is, if you do or say what you wish to, you'll be criticized; the fear of rejection, where you believe that if someone rejects you, it says terrible things about you; the fear of failure, where you believe that if you do not succeed, you will not be able to handle it. Fear of success is actually the fear of failure in disguise, as we will see.

Anxiety is often the fear of change, and that can prevent you from accomplishing the very goals that you cherish the most. Sometimes it's the feeling of fear itself that you fear most. Some people have a fear of death that is so strong that it prevents them from enjoying life.

Perhaps the most common form of anxiety is performance anxiety. See if you can find the common denominator in these situations: going for a job interview; asking for a promotion or raise; getting ready for a blind date or first date; having sex with a new partner; making a speech or presentation; dealing with authority figures; and taking an important test or exam. Performance anxiety is the underlying feeling that all of these things have in common; in fact a recent survey has shown these seven items to be the most common triggers of performance anxiety.

Performance anxiety in and of itself is not a bad thing, at least not totally. A little bit of it, as has been shown, can make you aware that some self-monitoring may be appropriate, so it can actually improve your performance. Performance anxiety only becomes a problem when it hurts your performance.

Let's take a look at how this happens. Say that you're going for a job interview. A little bit of anxiety is actually going to help you; it'll keep you on your toes. But if your anxiety becomes too visible to the person interviewing you, you could come across as being unsure of yourself. The net effect could be that you blow the interview.

The same would occur with taking a test. A little bit of anxiety is actually optimal here, but too much anxiety will often make you forget the answers and make failure—the very thing you fear the most—come true.

Likewise, I'm sure you've seen the Woody Allen caricature of the nerd on his first date, who bumbles so much that you wonder why his date hasn't left. (Sometimes she actually does.) That's performance anxiety at its most extreme; like most forms of anxiety, it can become a self-fulfilling prophecy.

Practically always, underneath performance anxiety is a mental process that we call *catastrophizing*. That's where you have it firmly planted in your head that the worst possible outcome will occur, and you go one step further and say to yourself, "That will be a catastrophe. I won't be able to handle it. I won't be able to live it down. It'll be just plain awful."

Sound familiar? To the extent that you have these attitudes, your anxiety level will predictably rise and your performance will decrease. For instance, in the case of sexual performance anxiety, which results in impotence, we usually prescribe a treatment which takes away any and all chance of failure from both partners. The result of this is generally an increase in sexual desire: because no performance is necessary, the anxiety dissipates.

Suppose you have performance anxiety around speaking. An idea may be to learn how to anticipate the worst, while being careful not to distract yourself by fearing it.

Maybe you're a person who mixes up caution with catastrophizing. The difference is that catastrophizing usually provides you with about ten times more caution than you'll ever need to pull off what you're trying to accomplish. By recognizing catastrophizing, you'll prevent it from becoming a self-fulfilling prophecy, and your performance will be optimal. Then whatever anxiety you still have can be experienced as excitement, which is a very positive emotion, rather than a negative emotion, with fear associated with it. Incidentally, excitement and anxiety are also physiologically identical. It's only the attitude you have toward that feeling that determines whether it's a positive thing or a negative.

Other ways to relieve anxiety include deep breathing and relaxation methods, which we'll talk about later on. Most importantly, anxiety will dissipate as you adopt a whole new philosophy that will enable you to think of life not as a performance, but as a set of exciting challenges.

A mental expression of anxiety that also has its own unique characteristics is worry. Worry is a feeling of uneasiness in the mind. Don't ever let anyone tell you that it's never beneficial to worry, because sometimes it helps you to evaluate a new course of action, but worry becomes a problem when you pretend that the power of thought can actually change something.

Worry has often been called *paralysis of analysis*. We think and think and obsess and obsess about some point until it feels as though the analysis itself takes on a life of its own and paralyzes us. Some people worry about anything and everything. It's rarely appropriate to worry about past actions, since our minds don't have a redo button like we have on our computers. We can't go back and redo something we've already done, but as we saw earlier with depression, how many times have you pretended that you could undo something that has already happened? That is beyond any human being's power.

If you were going to take a trip, but you were so worried that the plane was going to crash that you didn't even get on it, then worrying resulted in an action, although not necessarily a positive one. On the other hand, if you boarded the plane anyway, why keep worrying? As a passenger, you can't possibly stop the plane from crashing, but you can certainly make your trip miserable.

To address your tendency to worry, try this simple exercise. When worrying begins, get out a pencil and paper. At the top, write down the thing that you're worrying about, and make a list of everything that you *wish* you could do about the situation. Next, list all of those things you actually *can* do. Put the things you wish you could do on one side of the sheet of paper and the things that you can do on the other. Focus on what can be done, and plan a rational course of action to tackle the problem. Let go of the things on the other side of the list—the ones you wish you could do but can't. They are beyond your control. Don't devalue yourself for being unable to do what you have defined as impossible.

Earlier we talked about not defining things as impossible when they are merely hard. This is the exact opposite. If something is impossible and beyond your control—especially something that has already occurred—the task is to let go of it. I'm not telling you not to think about it, because what you think about is often out of your control, but you do have the choice of what you will pay attention to and what you will ignore. Sometimes it helps to treat those items you choose to let go of as unwanted thoughts. If you choose to ignore those thoughts and not to take them seriously, more often than you think, they'll burn themselves out.

One technique for stopping excessive worry involves putting a rubber band around your wrist. When you begin to have an unwanted thought, simply snap the rubber band, causing a slight amount of harmless pain. This is a very effective way to behaviorally attack obsessive and distracting thoughts.

## Overcoming Guilt

Few emotions are as worthless as guilt. Guilt means you've done something wrong; that's the legal definition, anyway. Without getting into a lot of judgment about what those things might be, if something has occurred that you feel guilty about, first remember the rule that says that undoing the past is impossible. With that in mind, how is it to your advantage to have that guilt?

On the other hand, your guilt may be, by your own admission, inappropriate. That is where you believe that you should have acted differently toward someone or something after the fact. Like all these conditions, look for that underlying *should*. What is it you're telling yourself you should have done? Are you making impossible demands on yourself again? Are you telling yourself there is something you should do that you otherwise wouldn't choose to do? Is there something you truly want to do differently? If the answer is no, then obviously your guilt is inappropriate, and you would best be served by giving yourself permission to let go of it.

Many people confuse altruism with things they do to alleviate their own guilt, or acting with some hidden agenda, or being hypocritical. In a relationship, when you're acting for the benefit of the other person, you're really acting on your own behalf, because in healthy relationships, the good things you do for the other person will come back to you. You may want to make a list of all those things about which you feel guilty, and then ask yourself, what is the demand that's behind that guilt? Is it appropriate? What are the advantages to holding on to this guilt? How is it serving you or the person or thing that you feel guilty about?

Chances are you won't come up with much that supports your feeling of guilt, and then those thoughts such as "What a rotten person I am for_____" (you fill in the blank) can become just another negative attitude that you now know how to alleviate.

# SIX

# Manage Your Stress and Avoid Distress

Stress is simply the pressure of daily living. That's right: To be alive is to be under some degree of stress. Stress can be generated either externally or internally, and how we handle our stress can have more to do with our health than perhaps any other factor.

Excess stress is called *distress*; thus distress is the amount of stress over and above what you can manage. Studies have shown distress to account for anywhere from 50 percent to 80 percent of all disease.

No matter how hard we try, we probably can't completely avoid the stress of daily living, but we can reduce it significantly by learning certain skills for coping. This can keep us on the right side of the invisible line separating us from the dangerous arena of distress.

First, let's understand what stress is, and then we'll talk about ways of managing it. Remember this simple equation: the difference between the amount of stress you have and the amount of stress you're able to manage is what causes distress. Our goal here is to eliminate that distress as much as possible.

Just as many people confuse frustration with low frustration tolerance, many confuse stress with distress. Stress in and of itself can be a motivator and a source of change and excitement. Some people are much better equipped than others to handle it, simply because their stress-management skills are more intact. For example, with a little bit of reframing, stress can motivate you to begin and complete a task that you've been putting off.

One of the main causes of stress is change. This could refer to job changes, such as a promotion, demotion, or transfer, or a change in your financial status, such as debts, loss, or even a substantial *increase* in income. Family changes, such as marriage, a pregnancy, a shift in family responsibilities, or someone leaving the house, even act as stressors, and in fact, usually do. Retirement is a very common cause of stress, even though the main symptom may simply be boredom, which you may think of as anything but stressful. Nonetheless, it's a change, and often an unanticipated one. And in fact, boredom is one of our most *unacknowledged* sources of distress.

Causes of stress can include any major lifestyle change: a new relationship or divorce, someone moving into your home, moving your place of residence, changes in the way you spend leisure time, or changes in social activities; also illness or injury, sexual difficulty, the death of a loved one, or another personal loss. If you think that's all, even predictable events, such as holidays and vacations, stress your system. In fact, every holiday season, callers to my radio program wanted to talk about holiday stress more than anything else.

In addition, there are numerous ways we put stressors on ourselves. Perhaps you tend to overplan each day, or you engage in so many activities or thoughts at the same time that you overtax your system. Excessive competitiveness and a dire need for recognition are all self-induced stressors. Being overextended, being involved in too many projects with difficult or impossible deadlines—and don't forget that compulsion to work while neglecting all other areas of your life—these are all attitudes that bring stress upon yourself.

Not allowing yourself to relax, or, worse yet, feeling guilty when you do relax is a big one. Low frustration tolerance and what's called *time urgency* or *hurry sickness* not only cause excessive amounts of stress, but also dilute your enjoyment of life. I'm not going to tell you to give them all up. I only ask that you recognize them and either choose them consciously or decide to give them up. And if so, do it only because you acknowledge that it's in your ultimate best interest to do so.

When is it in your best interest to give up these attitudes? Let me answer that question by describing to you the signs of distress. Consider these as warning signals: anxiety and depression, tension headaches, backaches, tics, muscle spasms, migraine headaches, abdominal pains and ulcers, colitis and other bowel disorders, tachycardia and other cardiovascular symptoms, and high blood pressure, or hypertension. Pounding of the heart, speech difficulties, indigestion, grinding of the teeth, unexplained aches and pains such as in the neck or lower back, general irritability, and accident proneness are usually stress-related as well. Distress may be the source of nervousness, sleeplessness, inattentiveness, feelings of fatigue, tightness of the chest, boredom, or an inability to slow down. It can also cause allergies, sexual dysfunctions, and an inability to concentrate.

Sometimes distress can be circular. For example, if you're under a lot of distress, you could be neglecting your most important relationships. That in turn could be causing you more distress. Furthermore, you may be putting yourself down because of your inability to handle those dilemmas. Dissatisfaction with yourself is highly correlated to depression, which of course is often a sign of distress.

Stress or distress can be confused with burnout. Although the symptoms are similar, usually *burnout* refers to a specific area of your life, such as your job. You know that it's job burnout when you feel a marked improvement in your mood when you're out of the work environment. In that case, sometimes a change of job or even a complete career change in a necessary next step, in order to restore optimal functioning. And sometimes merely a transition within the system in which you're working or a good, restful vacation can be the answer.

*Burnout* also applies to relationships, such as marriage. Stormy love relationships can certainly contribute a great deal of stress to life, but those that are characterized by indifference, especially when they were at one time fulfilling, are often found to be suffering from burnout.

If this is the case, and your relationship is one that you want to save, it's essential to begin communicating with your partner about this immediately. It's important to agree that this is what's happening. Next, talk about how things were different when you first got together, and try to work as a team to recreate that climate, so that perhaps even those sparks you once had can be reactivated. For a number of reasons, many couples find this very difficult to do without the help of a third party, such as a marriage counselor or a couples therapist. But when two people are willing to work together to rekindle a relationship, the success rate in counseling is very high.

How do we prevent stress from becoming distress? The answer lies in learning some new attitudes and habits that will result in a healthier lifestyle. Let's look at these one at a time.

Are you trying to have it all? If so, can you truthfully say that you've ever met a person who's actually reached that standard and actually had it all? I haven't. Remember the secret that practically all high achievers who avoid distress seem to know: with hard work and determination, you can have practically *anything* you want, but not *everything* you want. If your highest priority is having it all, then you're a perfect candidate for both job and relationship burnout, as well as untold amounts of distress. In addition to pushing yourself way too hard, chances are that your self-esteem will suffer as you experience the inability to reach this goal as a failure. With whatever you do accomplish, instead of enjoying the fruits of your hard-earned labor, you may negate the progress you've actually made.

## Strategies to Manage Your Stress and Avoid Distress

The key is to be satisfied with what you do have on one level while striving for the additional things you want on another level. Keep those goals realistic, and allow yourself to experience some satisfaction with what you have before pressing yourself for what you don't. (After all, what's it all about anyway?) This could mean putting off some things, such as having a child or relocating for advancement, or just plain giving yourself a break from the constant pressure to climb the ladder of success.

When you tell yourself that you must succeed in order to be a worthwhile person, chances are you're putting success above happiness, and after all, isn't happiness the purpose of success in the first place?

- Avoid hurry sickness. Allow for delays. Give yourself some slack in your schedule, and enjoy those times when you need to wait as a gift. I've found it very useful always to have a pencil and paper with me, so that I can jot ideas down whenever I have to wait. Perhaps this involves working toward enjoying your own company. If you can give yourself that gift, I can practically guarantee you that solitude will be one of your most favorite ways to spend time.

- Set priorities wisely while considering long-term versus short-term consequences. This can apply when taking on new projects as well as when being aggravated with something unimportant, or spending your time around individuals or circumstances that are meaningless. If your time is tight, a great habit could be to think about how meaningful whatever you're considering will be to you two or three years from now. Use this test to set priorities, and I can practically guarantee you that you'll be easier on yourself. Does the project or issue really matter? Sometimes you need to step back a bit and look at it objectively. Once again, do this as though you were advising someone else. If you find that it's difficult to achieve long-term meaning this way, then just say no.

Perhaps you will feel a little bit guilty at first, but remember that guilt is usually just a self-defeating attitude. With a little practice, you'll learn to ignore the guilt and be much more conserving and protective of yourself.

- Try reaching out to others around you when feeling stressed. Don't get hung up on an attitude that says that dependence on others is a sign of weakness. An example is an economic crisis. Let's face it: there are few things that can throw a family into as much emotional turmoil as an economic crisis, such as one caused by sudden unemployment, a large unexpected expense, a disability, or a major financial loss. But families who are able to stay together and avoid blaming themselves or one another are the ones who get through these situations with the least amount of distress, and they come out stronger for it.

- Keep a diary of your stressful situations and of negative feelings. Include all of the W's—who, what, when, where, and why—about whatever is going wrong. It's often helpful to have someone you can discuss them with. If there's an ongoing situation that you can't seem to resolve, get professional help. Consider reaching out for help as a power tool, not as a sign of weakness. Sometimes an objective party can help you to zero in on something that, no matter how long you wrestled with it, could have been very difficult for you to see clearly.

- Make a list of things that you feel good about and that make you feel good. When you're under the gun, take a look at that list so you can find some positive things that you can avail yourself of. Later I'll talk about ways of learning to relax, but you already know those things you enjoy: hobbies; playing golf, tennis, or another sport; getting a massage; going to your favorite museum; calling a friend; taking a sailing trip; playing a favorite video game; or going for a long walk in some pleasing environment, such as near an ocean or a lake or in a wooded area. Fall back on these things when you need them the most.

- Make effective use of your time by organizing your activities. Make your routine as stress-free as possible by trying to anticipate unexpected things that may come up. To have a schedule that is itself stressful only invites more stress.

Chances are you can't solve all your problems at once. Focus on what you can do effectively *now*. Also try to address your most difficult issues at a time when you're not overly bothered by them. Your thinking is much clearer then, and you're usually able to solve problems much more effectively.

- Take vacations regularly. Don't fall into the trap of thinking you're indispensable. No one is. Sometimes simply changing your environment will change your entire outlook as well. Short-term solutions, such as the use of drugs and alcohol, may make you temporarily *feel* better, but they're not without their side effects. Ways of natural relaxation can be just as effective and are a whole lot safer. Of course, there are times when prescribed medication is necessary, but self-medicating usually causes more problems than it solves.

- In addition to learning these positive attitudes, a complete program of stress management and burnout prevention involves exercise, nutrition, and relaxation. The type and amount of exercise you do is a highly individual matter, but twenty to thirty minutes, three times a week, of an aerobic-type exercise—where you bring your heart rate up to about 75 percent of your maximum (about 220 minus your age)—is thought to be the minimum for good cardiovascular conditioning. However, if you've been sedentary, before beginning any exercise program, please have a checkup, and exercise only with the knowledge of a physician familiar with your physical condition.

- Eating correctly and eliminating or moderating your use of sugar, caffeine, preservatives, artificial flavorings, red meat, highly processed foods, and fat are extremely effective in increasing your immunity to distress.

- Arguably the most important aspect of a good stress management program is to learn relaxation. Later I'll give you a couple of methods to do this, but first be aware of some other factors that will go a long way toward making stress work for you. Listen to your favorite music. Try to build fun into your daily schedule at work as well as at home. If this is not possible, something's wrong. Perhaps you're not in the environment you need to be in in order to have a happy life. Seek out those chronic sources of stress and do whatever is possible to make the necessary changes. If you start feeling anxiety coming on, practice breathing rhythmically and deeply. If you master this, you'll feel the stress just peel away. Breathing in to the count of five and out to the count of five is the simplest and one of the most effective on-the-spot stress reducers there is. Also, there are many great and free breathing apps you can put on your smartphone.

- In addition to exercising on a regular basis, do some daily stretching and find a form of activity that's fun for you and that will also get you active. If meditation or prayer work for you, make it a regular part of your daily life. Find that center within yourself that's safe and compatible with your ability to relax.

As I said earlier, so much of your life will fall into place if you don't take yourself too seriously. Even if you don't do any of the things that I've mentioned, accept yourself anyway.

At this point I'm going to teach you a very simple relaxation exercise that anyone can do practically anywhere for just about any length of time. The more you do this, the easier it gets.

Sit comfortably in a chair or lie down. If you sit, don't let your head fall backward or let your hands touch each other. Tell yourself that you'll take five deep breaths and go into a state of relaxation. Next, take four deep breaths, inhale the fifth breath, and say, "Relax now."

Exhale and tell yourself you'll let go of your tensions with each breath. Allow yourself to drift. If thoughts come through your head, just let them go by, like clouds in the sky. Don't pay attention to them, instead, simply put your focus back on your breath.

Stay here for as long as you would like. Five to twenty minutes is about the average. If you're concerned with time, it's OK to open your eyes, look at your watch or set a timer with a gentle chime, and close your eyes again until you want to stop.

When you're ready to bring yourself back, tell yourself that you'll count from one to five, and at the count of five that you'll come up feeling rested and fully refreshed, and that you'll remain awake, alert, and fully rested until you're in bed and ready to go to sleep tonight.

When you are ready to come up, simply count forward from one to five. At the count of five, your eyes will open, and you'll be fully refreshed, back in the room and ready to continue your day.

# SEVEN

# How to Change Habits

If you're like most people, you have at least one trait or habit you'd like to change. Most bad habits—those you know you'd be much better off without—represent something that stands in your way of success on the job, has some negative impact on your relationships, or may be negatively affecting your health.

Some habits even become sources of self-loathing: you constantly put yourself down for them and regard your lack of success in changing them as inexcusable weaknesses. So an additional negative by-product of that bad habit is that you may even think less of yourself for having it.

As we saw earlier, attitudes are thinking habits. Of course, they can be positive or negative. They can enrich our lives or be self-defeating. So can behavioral habits.

Much of your success on the job is probably due to positive work habits that you formed over the years. How orderly you keep things is based on your habits, as is your tendency to be early or late, and even how you eat and sleep.

Negative habits, however, are the ones that seem to concern us the most. They result in self-defeating behavior, which includes anything you do, consciously or unconsciously, to get in your own way, to undermine yourself, or to sabotage your own goals.

Habits are learned. That means they can be unlearned, and new ones can be relearned. With negative habits, the first step is to know the "enemy." This means to identify the habit in detail and visualize what it would be like if you were able to overcome it. Perhaps you can start now by asking yourself exactly what it is that you would like to stop or start doing. Behind every habit that needs to be changed, there's an attitude to be challenged or learned as well.

If you're trying to stop smoking, undoubtedly you've heard that smoking is an addiction, and you can become chemically dependent on nicotine, but isn't it really your attitude that perpetuates that habit—"I can't stand it if I don't have a cigarette," or "I'll never enjoy social events as much if I can't be puffing away," or "Certain activities aren't as much fun unless I'm smoking while doing them"?

That's right. It's that attitude we now know as low frustration tolerance that ultimately powers your habit of smoking.

Suppose you're trying to lose weight. I can't think of anyone I've ever met who's complained about overeating who didn't know that you gain a pound for every 3,500 calories you consume over and above what you burn up. Of course, there's no shortage of diet books, so we also know it's the amount and type of food you eat that determines not only your weight, but ultimately your health.

Let's look at the attitudes that are usually connected with overeating: "I must have that piece of chocolate cake," or "I deserve this pizza," or "I'm powerless to resist something that's put in front of me that I want, regardless of how much I'll regret it later." It's possible and even likely that you tell yourself these things without even realizing it. Think of them as automatic thoughts.

So just as our habits occur automatically, so do the attitudes and thoughts behind them. In fact, you could probably even think of a number of attitudes you have and things you tell yourself about smoking or overeating that are quite unique. Your unwanted habit has probably operated for a long time, perhaps before you even realized it was problematic. For example, if it's your habit to procrastinate, the first step is to acknowledge that you procrastinate. Then, when you do it, at least you're doing it consciously instead of automatically.

This is often the hardest part of changing self-defeating habits, since they may have become so ingrained in your nature. In fact, we even refer to habits as being "second nature." As self-defeating as they may be, there's comfort in them, because they're so familiar. I refer to this attitude as a *comfortable state of discomfort*. So as soon as you begin to change, you'll probably experience some discomfort until the new, chosen way of being becomes as second nature as the habit that you're trying to change.

Let's look at some other common habits and the attitudes behind them. If you're a crash-prone driver, perhaps it's your attitude that "people should stay out of my way," or "it would be terrible if I were five minutes late," or "driving a car is so boring I can't stand it, so I must get in there and hurry, even if the consequences of hurrying far outweigh any possible advantages."

If you're someone who habitually interrupts others, perhaps it's because you're telling yourself, "What I have to say is much more important," or "If I'm not being listened to, then I'm not being approved of," or "I deserve to be paid attention to and anyone who doesn't has committed an unforgivable sin."

The habits of procrastination or failing to eliminate clutter usually have behind them the attitude that "This is too overwhelming," or "Sure, I'll be sorry later on, but for right now, it feels so good to be doing something other than that dreaded task."

Some habits are simply expressions of anxiety, such as fidgeting, chewing pencils, tics, and twitches. Many habits are also blind spots—things that we do without even realizing it, but which are very noticeable to others. Even with blind spots, usually you can recognize enough benefit to see how it's to your advantage to change.

Our blind spots are, in fact, those parts of ourselves that are very obvious to other people but which we ourselves may not be aware of. The classical example is bad breath. It often takes someone else literally close to us to point out something we should attend to but may never be able to recognize on our own.

Let me go back to a question I asked at the beginning: when it comes to habits, what have you identified that's in your best interest to stop or start doing now?

## Strategies to Change a Bad Habit

To change a bad habit, first identify it in as much detail as possible. What thoughts reinforce it? What are you telling yourself that justifies it? Why do you even want to change it at this time? This why question is important, because without clearly understanding your motivation, change probably won't happen. When did it begin? Is there any particular person, place, or thing that triggers it? Are you ready to make the commitment to do whatever is necessary to break this habit?

Answer all of these questions for each habit that you would like to break. Knowing what you're dealing with in that amount of detail is a major share of the battle. How would things be more *or* less different if you were success-ful in changing this habit? If your goal is to stop smoking, how would your life be more difficult without the crutch of cigarettes? Imagine the ideal situation of giving up your habit. You may want to close your eyes and visualize how you would feel if you were actually able to become free of it.

- Try to savor the positive feeling that comes from the fantasy of being without the bad habit. You may want to write down the images that come up, since they stimulate the feeling that is what you're striving for. When you can conjure up a positive image in your mind, you've established the power to give yourself a tremendous amount of reinforcement when you're fac-ing the inevitable but temporary discomfort of change.

- If you're trying to lose weight, imagine yourself at your ideal weight as though being overweight were a thing of the past, and you were feeling the rewards of your hard work in breaking bad eating habits right now. If you're trying to stop procrastinating on a project, imag-ine yourself having completed that project and reaping all the rewards both of finishing it and putting an end to your procrastination.

The next step is to develop a plan of attack. Use all the wisdom that's at your disposal to strategize how you can best effect this change. For overeating, this step involves planning your diet, establishing an allowable number of calories, and visualizing your progress for the first few crucial days and weeks. Imagine yourself advising someone else on the logistics of changing their eating habits. If you find this difficult, you may wish to seek advice at this point or do some reading on the subject. This is the technical part of the task. Point A was identifying the habit; Point B was the goal. What you're doing now is drawing the shortest possible line between those two points.

Sometimes it's important to break your plan of attack into small, manageable parts. For instance, you may be procrastinating on a project because you see it as over-whelming. But if you look at it as a series of smaller steps, each of which you can take without feeling overwhelmed, your attitude toward the entire project may prompt you to pleasantly feel that it's much more doable.

- To stop smoking, come up with a plan to go cold tur-key or taper off gradually. Some people find various types of nicotine substitutes helpful, while others plan stopping at a time when they're likely to be under much less stress, such as during a vacation or a long weekend. Make an ironclad commitment to yourself to follow your plan. Make sure to build in time factors, and then announce it to all the people around you who can act as sources of support.

Support is, for many, the most important step in changing a difficult habit. For some people, this might be a formal self-help group, while for others just having someone you could turn to during periods of frustration and cravings can make success much more attainable. Support is often the power tool that will help you to get past those difficult moments between the time when you've given up the self-defeating behavior and the time when change becomes automatic and second nature.

- You may also want to write up a behavioral contract specifying how you intend to attack your habit each day, and if you live up to it, how to reward yourself, such as buying yourself a small gift or doing something you enjoy but don't ordinarily take time out for.

- Sometimes giving yourself rewards, which we call *positive contingencies*, won't quite do the job. That's where negative contingencies, often a stronger source of motivation, come into play. A negative contingency is some form of punishment that you subject yourself to should you go backward. They're very commonly used as part of habit-breaking strategies. They could be as simple as doing something you don't enjoy, such as cleaning your house, staying at home on a night when you would ordinarily be going to a pleasurable event or a social activity, or even giving money to a cause that you thoroughly *dis*believe in.

- Positive and negative contingencies are custom-designed. I once had a client who had been through many forms of treatment in just about every kind of self-help group there is for losing weight. She was about fifty pounds overweight and claimed that she was powerless to stay within her chosen diet. After much discussion, we came up with a very effective negative contingency. It seemed that there was someone she felt very unattracted to who kept calling her up for a date and whom she was constantly turning down.

  She wrote this person a love letter and even put a stamp on it. We agreed that I would hold the letter and that the first time she did not stay within her weight plan, she and I would walk to the mailbox together and mail it. Needless to say, the thought of this individual receiving a love letter from her was so intimidating that for the first time in her life, she shed weight in a way that actually made me concerned for her health!

The fact of the matter is you can do it. You need only to find what positively or negatively motivates you. That is the role of contingencies. You may want to take a few minutes now to think about what some contingencies of your own, both positive and negative, may work best for you, to get the job done.

With all of this, it's still important to allow yourself a margin of error. If you slip or relapse, learn to forgive yourself again and again. It's that self-acceptance that will empower you to believe you can ultimately succeed, and that's the attitude that will help you to succeed the next time.

We are all fallible. This is a fact to be used not as an excuse, but as a reassurance when you've done your best and failed or simply not gotten the results you wanted. If you're still having difficulty, think about *secondary gains*. They are the reasons underneath the surface that keep your self-defeating behavior in place. Sometimes these are also called *higher-order problems*.

For example, if you're having difficulty giving up smoking, it could be that you literally use cigarettes as a smokescreen. With your smokescreen removed, you may be temporarily much more uncomfortable relating to people in certain social situations. Somebody once told me that he never worried about his future until he stopped smoking, because he didn't think he'd be around very long. He needed to come to grips with the idea of planning for a long life before he could stop smoking.

Many people who fail to stay on diets really fear other issues that losing weight may force them to face, such as losing the excuse to avoid meeting potential love partners or dealing with the intimacy that could follow.

One obese married man whose weight was jeopardizing his health told me that if he were to lose the weight he needed to lose, he feared that he would be seen as attractive by other women. New options would tempt him to leave his marriage, which at the time was not working well. However, once the issues in his marriage were addressed, he was able to lose the weight. Scenarios like this are not uncommon!

Allow yourself a certain amount of anxiety, and don't let that set you on a backward course. Listen to some of the many audio programs and countless books that deal with problems such as low frustration tolerance, perfectionism, stress, and anxiety. Changing a habit, especially a long-standing one, can trigger just about every emotion and form of stress known to humankind, but the good news is nothing can defeat you except your own tendency to declare yourself powerless and give up. This is one self-defeating attitude that is totally within your power to control.

A major part of changing your unwanted habits is acknowledging the payoff you're getting for continuing to have them. Once that is eliminated and you've identified the habits, established goals, developed a plan of attack, and gotten the support you need, you'll be amazed at how much power you have over things you may have thought were out of your control. And most importantly, once you master this attitude, you can apply it to any area of your life.

# EIGHT

# Building a Positive Self-Image

Self-image is a concept that's racked with ambiguities. For one thing, the human being is such a profoundly complex organism that there may be no accurate statement that could describe the totality of that thing we call the *self*. After all, if you add up all the beliefs, behaviors, attitudes, qualities, and attributes that we can say represent some part of us, you wind up with an infinite number of traits. Some psychologists argue that it's mythical even to talk in terms of self at all, since so many millions of components go into this wondrous being we call the self. What is it anyway?

Instead of getting highly philosophical about it, let's just acknowledge that each of has our own definition of the person we view ourselves as being, and the highest compliment we can pay to what we'll call the *self* is simply to *accept* it. That means accepting yourself with all of your strengths, weaknesses, shortcomings, lovable and unlovable traits, habits, attitudes, thoughts, and feelings—all the ingredients that go into making you the person you are.

Does that mean that we close ourselves down to improvement? Absolutely not, because when you can distinguish between that total organism called the *self* and the traits and behaviors that you want to change, then change is possible, because you've defined it as being possible. That is the attitude that will make self-acceptance work for you.

Self-acceptance, or the lack thereof, is formed in early childhood. Parents, teachers, and others who are responsible for us often make the mistake of addressing us with global terms when what they really mean to do is to correct our behavior. For example, parents correct children by making overgeneralizations such as "You're a bad boy," or "You're a bad girl," rather than by specifying the behavior they're trying to correct. Thus we learn—erroneously—that our mistakes reflect on us as a total person rather than simply on what needs to be corrected. For this reason, many people develop an attitude of putting themselves down whenever they don't measure up to some standard.

Although it's possible and even common to say that you may have been carrying around a poor self-image since early childhood, the good news is that you can acquire a positive self-image at any point in life and very quickly.

The main thing that's necessary is for you to refuse to put yourself down anymore.

One of the most common myths about self-image is that it can't be changed at all. Let's look at this myth. Many people tell me that they've been down on themselves as long as they can remember, referring to events that took place in childhood. But if you believe your destiny has been determined by what happened to you as a child, let me suggest that that attitude is only going to cost you. I've seen people who've had incredibly traumatic childhoods or who've been victims of unspeakable abuses during their most vulnerable years, yet who somehow have been able to come through with a positive self-image.

By the same token, I've seen others who talk glowingly about their childhood. In some cases, childhood could have been the most cherished time in their lives. Some people can point to practically no childhood trauma at all, but still have problems with their self-image, however happy, normal, or benign their childhood may have been. As I've observed many times and over many years, when helping countless people with self-image and self-confidence, poor self-image is an attitude that can begin regardless of your background and then take on a life of its own.

Many believe that only years of therapy can undo the factors causing a poor self-image. Even if you tried the longest of long-term psychotherapy which focuses on childhood trauma, several times a week for years and years, worked through all your childhood traumas, and became free of your past hurts, the best thing you could hope for is to have the self-image you would have had if your parents had raised you perfectly—a standard I've never seen in real life. In any case, you can shortcut the process considerably by developing that attitude now and simply refusing to put yourself down anymore.

This does not mean you can't be critical about your behaviors, beliefs, attitudes, emotions, and other traits, because after all, growth as a person depends upon recognizing things that need to be changed and making those changes. But by refusing to put your total self down anymore, you are simply refusing to overgeneralize. That's nothing more than accepting the fact that no statement directed at the total self can really be accurate.

There are other, subtle ways of perpetuating a negative self-image. Perhaps you only focus on your failures and not on your accomplishments. No matter how much you accomplish, you don't give your accomplishments anywhere near the recognition that you give those areas of your life where you believe you have not measured up.

Perhaps you believe you're a victim, or that life has passed you by. Victimhood is an attitude that results when you don't take much responsibility for where your life is right now. Instead of turning that disdain on yourself, you may blame other people, projecting a negative self-image onto others that you believe have somehow held you back.

Some people devalue their accomplishments. They act as though they were impostors, who didn't really accomplish the things for which they rightfully deserve credit. This attitude comes from operating under the assumption that you are, at best, merely acting as if you were competent and as if you had the power to pull things off.

When you stop and think about it, though, it's not very likely that you're an impostor, because in the final analysis we can only be ourselves. In fact, I defy you to be anything that you're really not. Even if you make a living doing impersonations, in reality you are only yourself doing an impersonation; you're not being someone else. So if you find yourself devaluing or denying your accomplishments, stop right there and take them back. They are yours, and no one can take them away from you—except of course you. If this sounds familiar, think of how much more you could enjoy if you refused to consider your successes flukes and to constantly tell yourself things such as "I should have done better."

You could be putting yourself down simply because you believe that people around you should care about you. When they don't, you ally yourself with them. Thus you devalue yourself simply because you haven't gotten the approval of some other person.

Let's face it. There's probably always going to be somebody who will deny you love and approval. To the extent that you define yourself as unlovable, you are not only allying yourself with your detractors, but you may also be negating the feelings of the people who really count—that those who do love and care about you. It's unrealistic and perfectionistic to expect such wholesale approval.

Perfectionism, or trying to accomplish the impossible, not allowing yourself to make errors, along with that unattainable goal of having it all, is the perfect recipe for regret and frustration. Perfection keeps you from enjoying the success you do have, until you achieve that unattainable perfectionistic standard, which to my knowledge nobody ever has. It will keep you from enjoying the successes you do have, because you will constantly devalue yourself for not meeting some other goal. Most people believe the adage that to err is human, at least intellectually, or as it applies to other people or to errors that don't particularly bother them. The key to having a positive self-image is simply to accept yourself, warts and all.

All of us have certain traits that are positive, negative, or even neutral. I've had many people tell me that they did not like themselves until their self-concept was challenged, but I can't think of anyone who, when pressed, couldn't point to something about themselves that they cherished. By the same token, those who talk of liking or loving themselves can just about always tell you about certain traits that they would rather be without or downright dislike about themselves.

Building a positive self-image is nothing more than substituting some new attitudes for some old ones. When negative ones start coming into effect, consider them old habits that simply need to be challenged.

## Strategies to Replace Self-Defeating Attitudes

Here are a few new attitudes you can use both to challenge and to replace those self-defeating ones.

We all have things that take a little longer to grasp than we'd like them to. Comparing your inability to measure up to someone else's perceived strength will probably leave you needlessly feeling inferior. Don't compare your insides with someone else's outsides. Everyone is, in his or her own way, vulnerable. You may be comparing yourself to a person who is simply successful in getting the image across that they want you to have. Maybe it's real, and maybe it's not, but no image someone projects to you is ever a reason to diminish yourself.

- Don't be afraid to unleash your creative energies, which include those areas in your life where you're different. People may try to defeat you, but don't fall for it. In the end, you are the only one who can defeat you. Remember, no one can make you feel inferior without your consent, as Eleanor Roosevelt said a long time before the concept of self-esteem was in vogue.

- Your insights will increase your self-acceptance. They can make practically any problem a no-lose situation, because if things turn out right, you'll know how you've won, but if they don't, you've still learned a great deal. Insight will give you the wisdom for going forward and even more importantly, teach you that you *can* handle whatever it was you dreaded.

- Stop globally rating yourself. Remember the self cannot be legitimately rated. There is no standard by which we can rate ourselves as entire persons. We have certain characteristics that are great, other characteristics that can use improvement, but the self, to the extent that it exists, simply *is*. It cannot be spoken of globally without making that gross error of overgeneralization.

- There is no one whose love and approval are absolutely essential for your well-being. We would all like to have as much love, acceptance, and approval from others as possible, but to the extent that you define your own worth by how someone else relates to you, you've made yourself a psychological captive of that person. This principle can apply to a spouse or lover, children, bosses, coworkers, friends, members of organizations you belong to, and virtually anyone else you will run into during your life. As difficult as it may be to acknowledge at first, you are the only person whose approval your happiness depends on. As we will see later, you can learn to let go of just about anything else.

- Self-doubts are very much like anxiety in that the cure is to ignore them and to act as if they were not there. Although this may seem simple enough, many are prone to consider self-doubts as a kind of cancer: if you ignore them, they'll become all-consuming and eat you up. Therefore you may believe that self-doubts must be listened to and acted upon. Nonsense. I can think of no better definition for standing in your own way. This can affect any area of your life.

Notice I've avoided using phrases such as *liking* or *loving yourself*. I do so because these attitudes represent the same overgeneralization error that putting yourself down does.

Here are some more exercises you can use to build a positive self-image. Start taking stock of yourself. Make a list of your strengths and accomplishments. Look each one over slowly. Have you given yourself credit where it's deserved? Have you acknowledged those things you can be proud of?

It's OK to brag a little, especially to yourself, about the things you've accomplished throughout your life. When you start experiencing twinges of negativity toward yourself, use your list as a reminder that any negative statement that you globally make about yourself is inaccurate.

Also make a list of weaknesses you would like to improve on, problems you would like to resolve, and other areas for improvement in your life. Now start to approach them one by one, but without the attitude that you're powerless to change them. This is another subtle way of undermining yourself. Of course, you will get in touch with certain limitations, but you'll find that they are more the exception than the rule when you approach them without that stifling self-doubt.

Be aware of how you respond to compliments. Do you reject them because you think they can't possibly be true? Learn to accept them, even if you suspect they may not be. While you're at it, when you catch yourself in the act of doing something well, feel free to give yourself a compliment.

By the same token, make it a point to take in constructive criticism and feedback. This information can be invaluable if you don't allow yourself to get defensive about it. Once you've been able to accept the idea that it's not a condemnation of your entire self to have something that needs correcting, the feedback will help you to identify more of your blind spots as others see them, and will be a power tool for improvement.

If you're raising children, try not to make the same mistakes that may have been made on you. I remember once when my daughter was in nursery school, she came home very upset because her teacher called her a baby. When I asked her what happened, she said she refused to share one of her toys during an activity.

I took great pains to explain to her that her refusal to share meant that she was behaving in a babyish way, but that did not make her a baby. After all, I said to her, "if you were playing hopscotch, and you were acting like a frog by hopping, would that make you a frog?" At that, she laughed and saw the point. Then she agreed that her teacher was probably right, since by that age she certainly knew that not sharing was a babyish act. I can recall teaching her this concept many times throughout her growing up, and nothing makes me prouder of her than to hear her pass that principle on to her own children.

There's nothing more important that you can teach a child than to have a positive self-image. To the extent that this lesson is learned, it will spill over to every other aspect of his or her life and to yours as well.

# NINE

# Letting Go of the Past

Practically all of us have things we tell ourselves shouldn't bother us anymore, but regardless of what your logical mind says, you may have nagging feelings of anxiety, anger, and depression. They may have to do with something that happened a long time ago, or just recently. They can go back to childhood, adolescence, a difficult marriage or love relationship, an unpleasant work experience, or a bout of financial hardship. But regardless of what or when, past hurt and unresolved pain can negatively impact any aspect of your life. So, when the experience is over, but the feelings linger on, the task is to let go.

Sometimes unfinished business can be worked out with the "other person," but other times it can't. You may have unfinished business with someone to whom you have no access or who is no longer alive. Nonetheless, the feelings remain. The one option for resolution that's always available to you is to resolve it within yourself.

I believe that letting go is actually a skill. Some people know when the time is right to leave a person or situation, while others hang on way too long. Are you a good leaver, or do you tend to stick around long after it's in your best interest? When I talk about *staying around*, remember it's how you stay around emotionally that affects your attitudes more than anything else.

Sometimes regrets are healthy signs that something we may not have been ready to do at one time in our lives is ripe for exploration now. For example, do you tell yourself that if you had it to do all over again, you would do things differently? Maybe that's a question that's worth contemplating. Try this, make a list of all the things that you would do or look at differently if you could have a do-over. Chances are, that list you make will contain some great insight, if you take the time to be comprehensive. It may include some things that you took way too seriously then but you wouldn't take so seriously now; you also may come up with an item or two whose time has come. For example, many people go back to college, change careers, rekindle old relationships, or make other positive changes in their lives, that were motivated by a nagging but insightful thought. In that case, an inability or an unwillingness to let go is simply a healthy sign that you don't *want* to let go. Many people merely experience these thoughts as calls to do something differently. In a sense, these are dreams, and one of your highest responsibilities to yourself is to listen to those dreams and to act on them when appropriate. For many, this could be the wake-up call that prompts a career change or other major life change.

When you're plagued by things from the past, such as relationships that you know in your heart of hearts could never serve you, or when there's some loss that you're unwilling to move beyond, then what's called for is clearly the skill of letting go.

Love relationships are one area where many people have the most difficulty letting go. They could include a relationship that you decided to end or one that was ended by the other person and in which you had little choice. Let's look at some of the attitudes that can prevent you from letting go of an ended love. Let's also explore alternative attitudes that will allow you to move on to a more appropriate relationship.

If you were telling yourself, "I need that person back in my life, or another ideal relationship right now," or even "I need a partner in order to feel happy," these attitudes could be behind your feelings of panic, loneliness, depression, desperation, craving, or anxiety. A positive attitude would be, "I prefer a suitable relationship, as opposed to a poor relationship or no relationship at all, but I do not need a relationship in order to be whole."

Furthermore, do ideal relationships really exist anyway? I've never met someone who truly wanted their ex back, but I have met countless people who wanted their ex back without the flaws they believe made the relationship fall apart in the first place. Obviously that's totally unrealistic.

Another negative attitude results from telling yourself, "Taking charge of my life without a partner is too hard, and furthermore, I shouldn't have to put up with these extreme hassles." The result is discomfort anxiety, low frustration tolerance, and a lot of anger.

The positive counterpart to this attitude would be to say, "While this is a much more difficult time in my life than other times have been, *too hard* implies impossible, which it isn't, rather than difficult, which it is." If you're telling yourself it's impossible to go through this period without feeling extremely depressed, angry, lonely, or jealous (since everyone says it's perfectly normal to feel this way), then helplessness, depression, anger, loneliness, and jealousy are likely to result. A more positive attitude would say, "While it's perfectly normal for me to feel somewhat depressed, angry, lonely, or jealous, it's unhealthy, and I do have other choices. I'm perpetuating these extreme feelings through my own negative attitudes, and I can choose not to feel so upset by keeping levelheaded and not blowing things out of proportion."

If you're telling yourself, "After all I did for my ex-partner all these years, I'm owed a lifetime of happiness," or "I deserve better," then you're sure to have self-righteous anger. A more positive attitude would say, "While it is true that I gave a great deal in the relationship, and would have preferred that it last longer, I realize that giving does not guarantee the reward of reciprocity."

Another angry attitude would be one where you're telling yourself, "I deserve much better treatment for my acts than I'm getting. At the very least, I deserve fairness." A more positive attitude would be, "It's unlikely that my former mate will change his or her behavior toward me merely because that's what I want. Changes that a person makes for another person generally prove to be not only temporary but packed with ulterior motives. True change comes because of one's own desire to change. By working on my own anger, it's possible that my ex's attitude will change, but it's certainly not a given. Therefore these demands are in my best interest to give up. Then I can get on with my own life much more easily."

If you're feeling shame, guilt, and depression, it could be because you're telling yourself, "I have failed," or, worse yet, "I am a failure." A positive attitude would say, "Perhaps the relationship failed to continue, but that hardly makes me a failure. In reality, relationships end merely because they have run their course. The moment that I accept that, I will be free to begin a more appropriate involvement."

You could be feeling hopeless about a new involvement, as well as generalized anger at all potential partners, if you're telling yourself things like, "All men or all women are alike, so I'm sure to be hurt again." A positive attitude would be to understand that by generalizing about all members of a given sex because of the way one person behaved, you'll only build a wall that'll prevent further relationships. Hopefully, you've learned enough not to make the same mistake. Don't blow it now by taking other and future potentially fulfilling partners off the table.

Another negative attitude is to tell yourself, "There will never be another as good as my ex; I can never replace that person," whereas the positive attitude here is to realize that there are many other fish in the sea.

I've seen scores of divorcing people with children torment themselves by saying, "I've ruined everyone else's life by leaving, and I'm a horrible person for doing so and for having acted so selfishly."

The alternative attitude here is to acknowledge that although it will be hard for others, if you made the choice to leave, you did for reasons that were highly valid for you at the time. Don't forget to acknowledge the unhappiness that brought you here in the first place. Demanding no regrets at any time is an awfully tall order to put on yourself.

Of course, if you continue to second-guess yourself, you could be saying, "I've made the wrong choice. Now I've really ruined my life." That attitude could also be behind your depression, hopelessness, or jealousy, especially if you're the one who has left the relationship and find that your ex has become involved with someone else and/or merely moved on.

The positive attitude here is to acknowledge that you're thinking with hindsight. At the time you made the decision, you were acting on the facts and desires you had then. Now it's time to stop self-doubting. When you do, you are free to get on with your life.

Another source of panic is doubt about how you will survive in the future without that relationship, but the reality is that no one knows what will become of them from moment to moment. Life is full of situations where we feel like fish out of water. You adjusted to them before, and you'll adjust to this too, as long as you don't convince yourself that it's not within your power to do so.

Finally, when ending a love relationship, you may fear the rejection of others who have even stronger feelings about your relationship ending than you do. Some people may judge you harshly, but hopefully those who really matter will accept the situation, as long as you do.

On the other hand, some people may never accept this, and that may be disappointing as well, but since you're powerless to change their thinking, it's best to focus on a very important question: whose life is it anyway?

Remember, the capacity to love or enjoy life without a relationship belongs to you, not to the person from whom you've separated. The responsibility to let go of a relationship is yours. It's not the other person's responsibility to free you.

Those who can't let go often make one of two errors. One is to get prematurely involved in a new relationship. Rebound relationships usually serve little purpose other than to act as anesthesia in getting you over the pain of your last one. That's one reason that rebound relationships rarely last.

The other common error is to avoid new relationships completely, in order to avoid any possibility of getting hurt again. Negative emotions serve as a kind of protection from this; that's often why people cling to them. But if this is the case, those are walls that you have erected, so they are walls that you can tear down.

Any loss can trigger a grief reaction. Sometimes the pain is so great that your only relief is to deny that it's there, but denial only provides, at best, temporary relief, because underneath it are the angry feelings, perhaps of betrayal and disappointment. These can be directed at an institution that has discharged you from your job, or at anyone for any reason—even at a person in your life who has died. Then, of course, there are feelings of sadness, due to missing whatever it is that you've lost, even if it's something that you would never want back. Next come feelings of fear, terror, panic, and abandonment. What do I do now? How do I get my life together?

The next natural stage in the grieving process is to begin to problem-solve and to look for new solutions. If you're replacing a job, you'll need to begin making up résumés. If it's a love relationship, you'll begin thinking about your future and when you'll be ready to become available again. This is the beginning of your healing process. Then comes the acceptance of what has happened and the realization that you can't go backwards. At that point, you're free to make new attachments and to begin permanently healing by forgiving (if forgiving is in order). Then as soon as you're ready, it's time to declare yourself renewed or even reborn as your life takes new shape.

Some people have a great deal of difficulty forgiving. Indeed forgiving has many different connotations. Many find it difficult because they believe that forgiving means excusing what the other person might have done.

Instead, think of forgiving as something you do for your own benefit. Forgiving helps you to accept a situation you can't change, let go, and move on. It simply means that you stop blaming so that you can let go of negative feelings. Revenge might feel freeing, but holding out for revenge only keeps you hooked.

You can certainly even forgive someone without even telling them you've forgiven them. Remember that throughout life, there will be many people who will not meet your expectations, and there will be many disappointments. Although there is no particular reason why you may have lost out on some things, there's also no particular reason why certain things may have worked out for you. That's the reality of life!

## Strategies That Will Enable You to Let Go

Here are some additional things to keep in mind for developing attitudes that will enable you to let go. Watch your tendency to paint a past experience as either all black or all white. For example, with an ended love relationship, when you can remember both the good times and the bad times, then you're moving toward letting go.

If you're thinking in purely negative terms, realize that you're probably making that overgeneralizing error again. After all, if the individual from whom you were separating were that bad, you'd be so glad to have him or her out of your life that there would be no ambivalence at all. The anger is often associated with a part of the relationship that you're unwilling to acknowledge, that speaks to the good times you miss, no matter how bad the rest of it might have been!

By the same token, if you're remembering something only in positive terms, think about the things that made the relationship end. It may also be helpful to focus on the routine of daily life with that person rather than just on those unforgettably wonderful events that you cherish the most.

- When thinking about a former relationship or looking back on any past experience, don't make more of it than it was, and don't make less of it than it was. Look at the situation realistically. People close to you can often help you to do this. Remember the greatest healer of all is the truth.

- Sometimes even ending a very short-term relationship can cause you to experience as much pain as it would if you had been together for thirty years rather than thirty days. If this is the case, ask yourself whether the wound you feel is really a heart wound or just an ego wound that you're building way out of proportion. Ego wounds can feel like real losses, just as infatuation can feel like real love, but they're also illusions. By simply realizing what it is, the pain will often dissipate much faster.

- When someone close to you dies, remember that part of the process of letting go is to feel the sadness and grief. Healing occurs when you purge those feelings out of your system. Let yourself cry and feel the pain. There are few times in life when support can be more crucial.

- There's no compensation in this life for misfortune. That's unfortunate, but if you feel like a victim, realize that things are rarely as personal as they seem. In reality, others usually act in their own self-interest, and in the course of achieving their goals, you may sometimes get hurt. Often that's merely a by-product. Look out for your own self-interest, and stop preoccupying yourself with the anger that comes from the attitude that someone's victimized you.

- Another solution may be to confront someone in your life, perhaps a parent, an old lover, or someone else who does not have the same relationship with you now as they once did. Sometimes by talking over unfinished business, you can not only resolve it, but come to a new perspective that you might not have had on your own.

- Here's an exercise in mentally "dropping out" that I personally do often: I make a list of all the things in my life that are going on right now. In addition, I list all the people with whom I have constant contact. Once my list is complete, I go down it and think of what it would be like to let go of each item or person, and then rechoose those I want or need to be a part of my life. This exercise reminds us that even though we tell ourselves we wouldn't have chosen certain things, in reality, we are the product of our choices. It's quite a source of empowerment to know that whatever you haven't let go of, you've chosen.

- Here is another thought-stopping technique. Once you have decided to let go of something, if you continue to get residual thoughts about it, consider them to be merely unwanted thoughts. Use the rubber band that we talked about earlier. Give yourself a snap when you have an unwanted thought. For some people, instead of a rubber band, simply saying "Stop" to themselves can do the job.

Here's one final exercise in letting go. It will help put you in touch with some of the unresolved feelings you may have toward people in your life, past or present.

Close your eyes and imagine in your mind's eye the people in your life right now who are important to you. Just let them go through your mind's eye, almost as though they were appearing on a movie screen. Be aware of any feelings that come up for you.

Next, go back a year, and picture in your mind's eye the people who meant the most to you then. In many cases, it'll be some of the same people you visualized before. In other cases, it may be someone or even many with whom you presently have no contact at all but who were still quite important to you a year ago.

Again, become aware of the feelings you experience, and for a second reconnect with some of those people who were most important to you then. Be aware of anything that may be unfinished with them, anything you might want to ask or say to them.

Now go back five years. Again, picture those people who were most important to you then and played the most prominent roles in your life. Take note of who is the same and who is different, and become aware of any feelings that you may have triggered. Be aware of anything that may be unfinished with any of these people and of anything you may want to say to them.

Now pick another time in your life, sometime between five years ago and childhood. Picture in your mind's eye the people who were most important to you at that time. Be aware of any feelings that may come up. Be aware of anything that may be unfinished with them, anything you may want to say to them, or anything you may want to ask.

Finally, go back to your childhood or to as early a time in your life as you can remember. Again recall the faces in your mind's eye of the people who were most important to you at that time. Be aware of the feelings that they bring up for you and what you would like to say to those people as you remember them. Be aware of anything that may be unfinished, anything you may want to say to them, or anything you may want to ask.

Open your eyes now and take some notes. What have you have discovered about some of the people in your life that may be unfinished? What would you like to talk to them about, tell them, ask them? What feelings would you like to let go of? Take note of any regrets as well as any moments that you cherish.

Now ask yourself, "What do I need to do within myself to let go of any of the negative feelings I still have?" Focus on any attitudes that still give you a difficult time letting go of. Ask yourself, "To what advantage is it for me to hold on to these negative feelings?"

By now you know that you can choose the feelings you wish to hold on to and those that are very much to your advantage to let go of.

As I said earlier, letting go may involve working something through in the present with the person involved, if that person is available. These are all choices open to you. Regardless of when the event in question took place, remember that nothing can be as exhilarating as letting go of excess baggage, and there is no better definition of excess baggage than a negative attitude that continues to defeat you.

# TEN

# Effective Risk-Taking

Think for a moment what you could accomplish if you had absolutely no concept of failure, no concept of danger, and no need to adhere to those abstract notions that we call societal norms. If you could remove all those built-in limitations, what would you do differently?

Now think of someone you know who's successful or someone you admire. Probably the thing that you admire the most about that person is his or her willingness and ability to take risks. After all, aren't the heroes of our time those people who have been able to free themselves both of the expectations of others and their own preset notions, and then blaze new trails? When we go to the movies, aren't we often paying someone on the screen to do in his or her life the very things that we hold back from doing in ours?

There was a great movie once. It was one of Peter Sellers's last ones, called *Being There*. The main character was a simpleton by nature but had never learned the concept of anxiety or limitations. As a result, he was able to accomplish great things, far exceeding everyone's expectations, but expectations weren't really a problem for him, since he had none. No one had ever taught him to have expectations or to see any goal as being out of reach.

Don't we admire James Bond and other heroic characters who take risks to the extreme? Of course, risk-taking is not to be confused with thrill-seeking. With the latter, you may even place your life in unnecessary danger in order to experience the intense excitement of fear. Thrill-seeking is sometimes even used as a way of acting out depression.

So we need to look at the point when taking a risk is prudent, and when is it wiser to play it safe. These are questions that we all need to evaluate throughout our entire lives.

In looking at the attitudes necessary for learning effective risk taking, assume for now that you are the one who's designed the limitations by which you live, not someone else, and that the risks we're talking about don't involve life-or-death danger. Examples include confronting your boss when you believe he or she is wrong; approaching someone you would like to meet, perhaps a person you're attracted to; being assertive with a waiter or waitress who's either overcharged you or given you unsatisfactory service;

going to a party where you don't know a single soul, and somehow getting yourself included; and expressing views that are different from those of a group with which you are having a discussion.

I'm sure you can add to this list. You may want to do that now by thinking of some of the risks you've wanted to take but stopped yourself from taking. What was the perceived threat, and was the threat realistic? Were you telling yourself that if you tried, you might fail, and that that would be something you wouldn't be able to stand? Or that you would look ridiculous? How did you hold yourself back? Did you tell yourself that things were not so bad the way they were, or that they would change automatically without you taking the risk?

If so, are these just rationalizations or excuses, or do you really believe them? Later on, we'll challenge all of the excuses and many more, but first let's look at a major attitude that can hold us back from prudent risk taking and moving ahead in almost any area of life.

Each of us has a comfort zone. I'm not referring to a physical space, but a state of mind. In this state of mind, there are few or no surprises. If you enjoy your life exactly the way it is, then you've managed to get into a positive comfort zone, but there's also such a thing as a negative comfort zone.

Think about certain areas of your life, things about yourself, that are not to your liking, that you would advise your friends or children to do differently. Yet those things have somehow become a part of your comfort zone. Although you don't like them, you give up the temporary discomfort of change in favor of this imaginary net of safety.

It sounds like I'm describing a rut, doesn't it? Well, staying in your negative comfort zone, or what I previously referred to as a comfortable state of discomfort, is exactly what a rut is.

The great humanistic psychologist Abraham Maslow said the life process is one of choosing between the path of safety and the path of risk. How many times in our lives do we come up to that fork in the road?

One way to go represents safety, the known. Perhaps, this could be the job you have now, which doesn't have a lot of advancement attached to it. The other option is the risky one. You don't know where it's going to lead. Perhaps in this example, it's a better job opportunity, but one without the security you've become used to. The choice is always yours, but often it's made by default, because your fears of leaving the comfort zone get in the way.

Let's look at some of the fears and attitudes that may be keeping you chained to your comfort zone. Are you afraid of losing control, or of some dire consequence that's probably unlikely to occur?

Perhaps your fears are realistic. They could include losing your present relationship, if you were to bring up an unusually difficult issue; becoming involved in a love relationship and then losing it, a fear that makes many resist what could be a rewarding involvement; being rejected for reaching out to someone; being laughed at by someone that you're attracted to or that you wish would respect you; being alone or abandoned; having lifelong friends become cruel and rejecting when you need them the most; losing your job or your financial security; being looked upon as a failure. For some, the ultimate fear is death. Some people are so preoccupied with their fear of death that they greatly curtail the quality of their life. Possibly you avoid risk taking simply because you lack confidence in yourself to pull it off. As we've seen earlier, self-acceptance means accepting yourself with your losses, but these attitudes serve only to undermine our lives.

So our comfort zone is simply an attitude—one we have chosen to protect us and one we can choose to change. How many of the things that you fear will happen to you in your lifetime actually do occur?

Think about times when you were anxious about an event or something specific. Try to get a sense of whether the things you feared the most actually did occur. Undoubtedly you will find that often your fear was real, but in actuality how dire was that threat, even though you may have feared it quite intensely?

Now let's focus on a present issue—some way in which you are adhering to that comfort zone when you really would rather go in the other direction, toward genuine growth and change. What's the worst thing that could happen if you let yourself take that risk? Do you fear that you'll become overwhelmed, and that if you get just a little bit outside of your comfort zone you won't be able to handle it?

If so, take a few steps back and ask yourself, "So what? So what if I try and fail?" Chances are you'll come up with an answer or two, but you may need to ask "So what?" three or four times until you get to all the things you really fear. Do you tell yourself that failure is something you won't be able to stand, that you could be rejected and that rejection would totally destroy you, that you'll be embarrassed or humiliated, that other people around you will suffer? If you are telling yourself that last one, could you be exaggerating the impact on others that your risk taking would have?

I would like you to try an exercise I call the *emotional fire drill*. It's very simple, and you can do it quite often with practically any fear or issue. Imagine the absolute worst thing that could occur as a result of your taking a risk. In fact, exaggerate it to the hilt. If you're catastrophizing, imagine that the catastrophe has occurred, and that it's even a harder thing to deal with than anything that you could ever have suspected. Let yourself feel the emotions. See those other people around you laughing or having the reaction that you fear the most.

Now stop and ask yourself a few questions. How realistic is it that the catastrophic reactions that you have imagined will come true? Even if some of the things you imagined were to happen, would they be as bad as you may have feared them to be?

Remember the difference between realistic fear and anxiety. The anxiety feels very similar to fear, but fear presents a real danger, whereas anxiety is in fact an imagined danger.

Next, think through what you would do to deal with the situation, in as much detail as possible. If the worst occurred, how long would it have an impact on you? Is it really the catastrophe you feared? When you bring yourself back into the present, notice the change in your mood. Remember that the feelings that you experience are ultimately under your control. It's your thinking and your attitude that determines your outlook.

This emotional fire drill shows how it's your attitude that will determine your reaction to a perceived outcome, much more than the outcome itself.

Next, let's try the opposite. Think of a time when you took a risk and it came out in your favor. Think about how exhilarating that may have been. Now plug the current risk you're contemplating into that frame of mind and imagine things coming out the best possible way.

Imagine the reactions from the people you care about being sheer joy and admiration, at a crescendo pitch! Take a few moments to feel those good feelings and to know that they are just as much under your control and just as much a product of your own positive attitudes.

You've taken a potential situation where leaving your comfort zone, taking a risk, may have been called for. You've experienced it at its best, and you've experienced it at its worst. In reality, it will probably come out somewhere in the middle. Fortunately, life doesn't usually give us as many extremely negative consequences as we fear it will, or sadly as many extreme positives as we hope it will. So chances are that the last time you risked and it didn't turn out the way you wanted it to be, it wasn't really the catastrophe you imagined, and chances are that when things do work out positively, it won't be as exhilarating as you expected either; in fact, you may even be a little bit disappointed. But whether it turns out positively or negatively, you will have had an experience in risk taking that will make the next time that much easier.

That's right: taking risks is like any other habit. The more you do it, the easier it becomes. I have found that losses are even more important than wins, because they are the things that test us. They are the things from which we learn the most and gain the most insight. If you can keep that in mind, you can turn your losses into no-lose situations, because when you've lost, you've proven that you can handle it. If you don't let that undermine your self-confidence, taking risks will continue to become easier. This is what we call the *elegant solution*, and no one can take this attitude away from you once you've formed it. It brings with it the emotional muscle that's so important to have in leading a happy life.

In my experience as a clinician, those who are usually most ill-equipped to handle a crisis are those who have very little experience in losing. They haven't had the chance to develop the crucial emotional muscle that comes with meeting these ultimate tests.

By definition, a risk carries with it uncertain results, but isn't certainty an illusion? Think about it. What do any of us really know for sure anyway? Do we know for certain that we'll be alive five minutes from now? Of course, the probability is extremely high, but certainty is nonexistent. Those who wait for it before acting shut themselves off from the lion's share of the life experience—the one that comes from taking that fork in the road that may be risky, but in the end provides us with most of our truly growth-filled experiences and long-term joy.

No one can tell you how broad or narrow your comfort zone should be, or the amount of risk that you should take or be comfortable with. Like everything else in life, this is a choice that only you can make for yourself, but the key is to choose it consciously. That can only be done when you look at the attitudes that hold you back and the emotions those attitudes conjure up. Then decide whether to give into that part of you that craves safety—and that's OK too—or whether to open a new door that may lead to a richer and more fulfilling life.

# ELEVEN

# Setting Your Goals

There's probably nothing that can be more important in determining your ultimate success than the skill of setting your life goals. Notice I said *skill*, because goal-setting is a skill. As important as it is, it's a skill that many people never learn. Sticking to your goal requires some attitudes that will attack the tendency to sabotage your own efforts.

First, let's talk about what goals are and how we can set them. Most definitions of success say that it amounts to reaching the goals you've set for yourself. Of course, there's no universal definition of success; many who you think have achieved extremely high stature hardly consider themselves successes. Yet many whose achievements are quite modest feel very successful.

The difference between the first and second person is that the first person has not achieved his or her goal, and the second has. So satisfaction or meaning in life comes from committing to a goal and relentlessly working toward it to completion.

Many leave their lives to chance and then wonder why they don't achieve success, or they consider others who have as merely lucky or as having some gift or unfair advantage. But the fact is that unless you determine where you want to go, you will probably wind up somewhere else. Only then will you know that you're not living out someone else's goals or are stuck in some rut that you can't change.

Getting what you want in life is usually a matter of priority. Remember: you can have practically anything you want, but not everything. So in setting your goals, keep them realistic, but most importantly, find the time to enjoy what you *have* accomplished, because what you've already accomplished were yesterday's goals. Chronic dissatisfaction can result when you have a tendency not to recognize what you've already achieved.

Keeping those things in mind, clarify your goals by asking what you want more of. That question can encompass any and every area of your life. When you're thinking about your goals, some anxieties may come up, like the fear of failure and, what is even more sabotaging, the fear of success. In fact, those fears alone are the reason that many resist setting the goals that will help them to take charge of their lives.

So step one is once again to act as though you have no fear. Sometimes it can help to think of goal setting as though you were doing it for someone else and you didn't have to reach the goals or be responsible for the outcome; you may need this degree of detachment to let yourself be the architect of your future. If you become aware of your fears, put them aside for a moment. We'll get to them a little later.

What many people find helpful is to make up what I call a goal chart. You can take an ordinary piece of 8½" x 11" paper or use a spreadsheet on your computer or smartphone. Draw seven lines across and five lines down, giving yourself thirty-five blocks that you can fill in. Start at the top block on the extreme left, and write *today*. Underneath write, *next week*. Underneath that, *next month*. Underneath that, *next year*. Underneath that, *five years*. Underneath that *twenty years*, and underneath that, *life*.

|              | Goals for me | Goals for my family | Goals for my career | Whatever may be left |
|--------------|--------------|---------------------|---------------------|----------------------|
| Today        |              |                     |                     |                      |
| Next week    |              |                     |                     |                      |
| Next month   |              |                     |                     |                      |
| Next year    |              |                     |                     |                      |
| Five years   |              |                     |                     |                      |
| Twenty years |              |                     |                     |                      |
| Life         |              |                     |                     |                      |

On the top part, head the columns up starting with the second one over: *goals for me*. The next one, *goals for my family*. The next one, *goals for my career*, and put in the final column *whatever may be left*. It can be any pet project you have, a cause, or anything else in your life that you consider important.

Now you're left with twenty-eight empty blocks that give seven different periods of time, starting with today and going through to the rest of your life, and columns where you can identify your goals for yourself, your family, your career, and perhaps something else.

Put a general goal in each of these blocks. Goals for yourself could include some educational goal, getting married, buying the boat you've wanted, taking a certain type of vacation, or even retirement.

For your family, they could involve goals having to do with your children or others close to you. The third column, dealing with your career, can involve a job change, a promotion, or any career development that you would like to see happen.

The fourth column can be anything else that you think is worth setting a goal for. Think in terms of ideals, but make sure that these goals are achievable.

Most people find this exercise to be very enlightening. Some find it painful, because it conjures up self-doubts and fears, but at this stage, we're just letting those fears go in one ear and out the other, acting as if we're able to operate without them.

If the spaces are not big enough for you to write what you need to write, use additional paper or spreadsheet columns, but the important thing is don't let anything stifle you. Try to put something into each block.

Next I want to give you another exercise to help you to further visualize your goals. Visualization is perhaps the most powerful tool there is in setting goals, which are really visions. In fact, a law of visualization says you can't consciously achieve what you can't first imagine. Just about every breakthrough or achievement, whether in business, science, exploration, or any of the arts, started out as someone's visualization.

This exercise can be done for any of the time periods on your goal chart. Find a comfortable place to sit down and relax. Close your eyes and concentrate on your breathing for four or five breaths. Now think about an accomplishment that you're most proud of. Think of something that you've achieved that you may at one time have been full of doubts about, something you attempted in spite of your doubts, or something that you didn't even know was difficult until you tried it. In any case, think of something that you tried and pulled off with as much success as you wanted, if not more.

Get in touch with the light and happy feeling that that image conjures up. Now, using your goal sheet as a departure point, pick out any period of time, whether it be today, next week, next month, one year from now, five years from now, or twenty years from now.

Imagine yourself at that period of time having achieved all the goals you've set out for yourself. Become aware of the feeling of satisfaction once again, and take a look around you and see what is happening in your life. See your situation with respect to relationships, career, finances, and children. Think about the hobbies you may be cultivating. What's going on in that area of your life?

You've tapped into a place within yourself where you can go at any time to retrieve some invaluable data. What you're visualizing is a result of having achieved certain goals that you may not even be aware of now, but seeing them in this context can help them to become much clearer to you.

You may want to do this exercise often and for different periods of time. Have a pencil and paper handy, and take notes. Imagine how it can feel during those periods. You have no anxiety, because the things that you may be anxious about now have worked out the way you wanted. What you're doing is visualizing what is possible.

Open your eyes whenever you're ready, and look at the goals you would like to achieve. At this point, you could even be experiencing them as wishes. If you stopped here, people might call you a dreamer, but it's the next step that makes a transition between where you are now and where you want to be.

Now we're ready to spend some time crystallizing these goals. Start looking at them one by one and break them down into smaller subgoals. Many who fail to achieve goals do so because they don't deal with them in manageable pieces; rather they look at the entire goal as something that's overwhelming.

For example, if your goal were to become a lawyer, the first step is to collect information about law schools. Look at brochures, fill out some applications, take interviews, study for and take the entrance exams, arrange your financing, and get accepted. Then, of course, there are many other subgoals that will come between the time that you are accepted and the time you pass the bar exam.

Maybe your subgoal requires you to collect some information or talk to people who can help you to clarify what you have to do to reach your goal. Getting support and information from other people is an integral part of getting ahead. Almost any successful person can usually point to a whole array of people who helped them to get there. But you are the quarterback, and nothing is going to happen until you determine the moves. When you start to get off track, see whether the goal needs to be changed or whether you need to just give yourself a push.

As with habits, sometimes it's a matter of rewarding yourself for staying on track or punishing yourself for falling backwards. This may involve looking at the people you've chosen to be around you. Do your network and environment support your goals, or is it the opposite? Some people find it crucial to surround themselves with people who are more success-oriented and with whom they have some common goals.

In setting and achieving goals, it's not the logistics that people have the most difficulty with. Instead it's a matter of identifying and removing certain roadblocks. That's where the work of positive attitude training gets even more specific.

The two most self-defeating blocks are the fear of failure and the fear of success. Of course, the good news is that both of these attitudes can be overcome. But to the extent that you expect that you must always do well or you must do perfectly, you'll probably experience your goal as overwhelming. You may then fear failing to reach it, and if so, you may not even try.

The trick is to turn both success and failure into win-win situations. Of course, if you win, you've met your goal. That one's easy, but how about if you fail? Let's look at what failure means to you. Do you tell yourself that you're less of a person or that you are unworthy of succeeding? As we saw earlier, if you're putting yourself down, you'll try to avoid that feeling of failure at all costs. Instead, consider adopting some new attitudes about failing.

Often failure is the short-term price you pay for long-term success. Unless you're too busy downing yourself for failing, there's a ton of information to be learned each time you fail. Practically every successful person I've talked to has pointed to their failures as being the very vehicle that somehow, often inadvertently, gave them their formulas for success. I believe that failure is our best teacher!

Much learning comes from trial and error. Sure, life would be great if we could find a way to eliminate the error part, but it's rare to find a successful person who didn't have to display the courage of getting up off the ropes a few times before success kicked in. Failure also makes you appreciate success more when it comes. Chances are if you're determined to hang in there long enough with realistic goals, success will come. Sometimes failure is necessary for letting go of an unrealistic goal.

Next to the fear of failure, the most common reason we sabotage our goals in the fear of success. Now you might ask, how can anyone fear success? Isn't that something we all strive for? Fear of failure is much easier to understand, but if you're good at defining goals yet don't seem to reach them, it's possible that you're fearing success itself.

The fear of success is really the fear of failure in disguise. You fear that once you get to the next level, you'll fail, so it's dysfunctionally easier not to get there at all than to get there and fall down. Then when you don't achieve the goal, you simply tell yourself some version of, "I never got to it." For some, in the short run, this is an easier pill to swallow than trying and failing. Sometimes you even blame your own ineptitudes, circumstances, or lack of luck for not having gotten there, but the real culprit is the fear that you *will* get there.

Fear of success may kick in when you feel too guilty or unworthy to get what you want, or when success means giving up some kind of security that you now have. As we will see later on when we talk about making major life changes, many have found that success in one area of life leads to a crisis in another. A major promotion can become a family crisis if the entire family has to relocate, for example.

Fear of success is really a form of higher-order problem, one that brings with it secondary gains. Imagine yourself really succeeding. Be as specific as possible and become aware of the feelings that come up for you. If you can get into that visualization frame of mind, where you can literally see the sights and smell the smells of success, and the emotion that comes to you is one of anxiety, guilt, or doubt, then the fear of success is probably what's holding you back.

This is just another attitude, so once you recognize it, you can start working vigorously to change it. Here are some more positive affirmations that can help you to turn that attitude around: "If I get to the next level and fail, I won't fall part." Success and failure are all personally defined terms. "If I try and I'm satisfied that I made every effort, I will not pin the failure label on myself. Even if I do fail, and the word *failure* is appropriate, at most it can only be applied to the task at which I failed, not to myself as a person. I am as deserving as anyone else of the success that I've envisioned for myself."

When setting goals, it's important to make your life as balanced as possible. As we saw earlier, success isn't the whole answer either. It's important to cultivate relationships with the people that you care about the most and to work toward making them allies rather than adversaries in whatever you're trying to achieve. This way success, when it comes, will positively impact your relationships rather than paradoxically make you more estranged. In addition, you'll be much more assured of support, rather than having the people around you seeing your success as a threat or obstacle in their lives.

The manner in which you set and reach your goals will test you as perhaps nothing else will, but once you've mastered this skill, then you can truly say that you've taken your life into your own hands.

## TWELVE

# Beyond the Status Quo

It's quite possible to be very much the architect of your own life, to set goals diligently and stay on top of the fears and roadblocks to reaching them, yet somehow still feel that there's something missing. If this is the case, it could be that before you find out just what that "it" is, that thing that will bring you back on track, some major change or changes need to be made.

Let me tell you a personal story. Before becoming a psychologist, I was an accountant. In fact, I had gone through undergraduate school at night as an accounting major, and by the time I was in my early twenties, I was a senior accountant. What I thought at the time was the opportunity of a lifetime came along. I had the opportunity to buy the branch office that I was managing from the larger accounting firm for which I worked. So in my early twenties, I actually had my own accounting firm. Through a combination of hard work and some good breaks, the firm became very successful.

By the time I was in my mid-twenties, I had achieved goals that I had thought I would have been happy with twenty or even thirty years later. The firm was growing, I was making good money, and there was no end in sight. There was only one problem: I wasn't happy. In fact I was extremely bored.

My work had ceased to challenge me. I talked to a lot of people about this and got very little empathy. Most people couldn't see how I could be anything but extremely happy with my professional life, but soon I started thinking about making a career change. Psychology had always fascinated me, but I had never really entertained the thought of doing it for a living.

Most people I talked to encouraged me to go into law. With my accounting and business background, by getting a law degree, I would be a natural for practicing tax law. That would be a very easy and logical transition from having an accounting firm, but the thought of that depressed me even more.

I got little support at home. My wife, who was pretty satisfied with the way things were, discouraged me from doing anything different. We entered marriage counseling, and as a result I seriously explored the idea of finding out what I really wanted to do. For the first time, I started looking at psychology as a possible career, and I felt excited and challenged. The sacrifices, I knew, would be extremely great, both emotionally and in terms of income, and there wasn't a lot of support for making the transition, but the more I entertained the idea, the more I knew that no matter how much sense it made or didn't make, this was what I wanted to do. I firmly believed then, as I do now, that if I had one life to live, I was going to live it in a way that I would find fulfilling, and the life I was living just wasn't making the grade.

Over a period of years, I went back to school and got a master's and a doctorate. For the first couple of years, I ran my accounting firm on an absentee basis, and then I sold it. But in the interim my marriage ended, partially because it could not withstand the stress that this new direction put onto it. There were also other reasons why my marriage ended, but if my wife and I had one major philosophical difference, it was that she was not at all a risk-taker, and I was. In fact, we had an important disagreement at the very beginning of our relationship, when I went into my own practice, which initially resulted in the loss of a secure salary. The benefits of being self-employed soon outweighed any of the sacrifices, and the income more than sufficed, but that next major career change was a risk she could not understand my wanting to take.

The transition was a painful one on many levels, but if I had to point to one thing that I'm most proud of doing, it's making what for many seemed like an illogical change, but one that was crucial for feeling a sense of meaning in my life. By the way, things worked out many times better than I ever thought they would.

A very important part of the life process is to let yourself dream. Perhaps you've seen how you get into your own way, how you sabotage yourself, or how your fears get blown out of proportion. It's important to see that no change is out of the question unless you—and you alone—define it as such. Remember what we said earlier: that in the end, no excuses are accepted.

So think of a change that you would like to make, something that you believe would really make a difference in your life. It could be a job or career change, going into business, going to school, dropping out of school, quitting your job. Perhaps you're feeling trapped in a marriage, or perhaps you're contemplating taking a relationship to the next step. Maybe the issue is whether or not to have a child. Perhaps it's something that nags you in your thoughts, or something you dream about. Perhaps it's something that you might have done at one time in your life, but couldn't or decided not to do then. You hoped to put it to rest forever, but now you find that it just won't go away.

If you're in touch with a desire for change, see if you can become aware of how you're holding yourself back. Is your fear of change stronger than your desire to make it? Is there something that you'd like to change, something that each time you think about it, you feel more and more validated in your desire to make it, but you hold back on because of a desire to avoid the unknown or leave your comfort zone?

Maybe it's opening a Pandora's box, because often one major life change leads to many others. When I first started changing my career, I wound up seeing that before I was finished, I would be changing my entire lifestyle—becoming a single parent, a student, and a person in transition.

Yes, if you fear change, that attitude can keep you forever addicted to a status quo that you don't like. It can keep you in a relationship or marriage that isn't working, in a job or career that doesn't fulfill you, or in a part of the country or world that's not where you want to be. It can also make you resent anything you connect with that unwanted status quo.

Sometimes the status quo is treated like a sacred cow. If you do that, then possibly you're blaming things outside of yourself for your own fear of change. But changing involves courage, and, remember, looking change squarely in the eye and making it involves risks and the willingness to accept possible failure.

Sometimes it simply helps to act *as though* you have courage—pretend, if you will. Remember, courage is nothing more than an attitude and the willingness to act on it.

Let's talk about some specific major life changes, what can bring them about, and some things you may want to consider before making them. We'll talk about career change first. Many make career changes as a result of burnout. We talked briefly about job burnout earlier.

Burnout is usually experienced by people who have been most enthusiastic about and dedicated to their work. Indeed, those who burn out are most likely those who were, at least at one time, on fire. If you've felt that you were making an important contribution but that your field has built-in frustrations—conflicts with the people you serve, with coworkers, or with the system itself—perhaps this led you to feel boredom, stagnation, or apathy. At some point, you may not even feel like trying anymore.

Job burnout can be experienced as chronic cynicism, depression, hopelessness, low self-esteem, all related to your job or profession. Sometimes the situation is temporary, and you can avert burnout by looking at the problem at hand or just taking a break. At other times, a change of job or career may be called for.

There are a few questions to ask yourself if you're in this situation: Are you dissatisfied with your entire career, or is it just the specific job you're in? Perhaps you could find satisfaction in a related job within the same field. Is it a change in your environment or a change in your attitude toward your work conditions that's called for? Are you feeling a calling toward another field? Are you willing to get the education and pay whatever dues are necessary to make the change you're thinking about? How important are the golden handcuffs, seniority, retirement fund, and other benefits that you would be leaving if you made this change? How will it affect your family members and others you care about?

Have you planned out the steps from point A to point B, as we mentioned earlier when we talked about goals, or are you simply daydreaming? What impact will this change have on your life five, ten, twenty years from now?

What sources of support can you rely on in carrying out this change? If there are none, are you still willing to make it? Become aware of the things that come up for you as you ask yourself these questions. Be aware of what contributions you want to make for yourself, to your family, to your career or profession, and to the world. Do these questions I am urging you to ask yourself make the change seem more or less desirable?

Many of these same questions can be plugged into your thoughts about going back to school, relocating, or making changes in your family or major relationships.

Later we'll talk more about decision-making itself, but for right now, the idea is to determine whether to move forward or to give it up. It's just as legitimate to decide that a change you've been contemplating is unrealistic. Your only task then is to accept it as a mere fantasy and let go of it. The thing that's most important is that *you* make the choice.

If you're thinking about leaving a relationship, be aware of the following: for a relationship to begin or to continue, there has to be some degree of desire and/or effort on the part of both partners; but the decision of one person is all that is necessary for a relationship to end.

Assess what your relationship means to you at this point. Is there an issue that's been poisoning it that you've been unable to resolve? Have you left no stone unturned in trying to resolve it or to find other alternatives, such as couples counseling or therapy?

Can you imagine yourself happily in this relationship five or ten years from now, or does that thought utterly depress you? Have you discussed your feelings with your partner? If so, are they mutual, or are you the only one who feels this way?

Whenever you contemplate a major change, expect that there will be a period of transition. Transitions are simply the hellos and good byes of life. Hellos are beginnings and are often our happier times. The tricky thing about hellos is that they are often just as stressful as the normally less happy good byes.

Sometimes you may have been fearing the transition itself, and that fear can be blown way out of proportion. I couldn't count the number of people who have told me in my office that the actual occurrence wasn't a fraction as painful as the fear of it was.

Without transitions, life would become stagnant or at the very least predictable, but because transitions can be very stressful, it's prudent to plan them as methodically as you can. Use all of your goal-setting skills when doing this. The attitude that will help you the most is developing a sense of excitement for the transition, a sense of anticipation for what will come. Remember this will be physiologically identical to anxiety, except that the dread won't be there.

Instead you'll have the thought of happy anticipation. You're moving toward a course you've chosen. Visualize yourself making the change you've chosen and coming through with flying colors.

In fact, let me give you a specific visualization exercise. It's similar to the one I gave you in goal setting, only this one is designed to take you past the transition.

Again, close your eyes and concentrate on breathing for four or five breaths. Relive in your mind's eye a positive image from the past, something that's associated with success, something difficult you've been able to achieve, something that conjures up feelings of joy and happiness.

Next, go through your transition period, beginning with where you are now. Pretend you can simply jump over the stressful part and come out the other side, having successfully gone through the transition. Be aware of how you're feeling right now. Visualize it as completely and fully as possible and note any steps that may come to you about how you were able to pull it off as masterfully as you did.

Let yourself go ahead a year, five years even, and look back at today and feel pride for letting yourself make the decision and taking the risk that the transition demanded.

Try this visualization exercise for five or ten minutes at a time daily, making that end result exactly what you want it to be. When you're satisfied, open your eyes, and acknowledge the success you feel for having made the transition. Do this with the attitude that it's a done deal, and do it as often as you need to, in order to carry you through the transition.

When you're making transitions, it's always possible to hit an impasse. An impasse is an area where you get stuck. To illustrate this, simply take a piece of paper and write down a situation. It could be anything, even a problem or issue that's very minor. Write the problem down in a sentence or two, and draw a line underneath. Write down what the situation would be if the problem were resolved.

Now let that line on your piece of paper represent the impasse, the area where you're stuck, the difference between where you are now and where you would like to be.

Close your eyes and project yourself ahead five years. Imagine it's today's date five years from now. You've come through the problem or issue that needed to be resolved, the change you were looking to make, the transition you were struggling with, and it's turned out better than you ever thought it would. You've come through it with flying colors.

As the you of five years from now, write a letter to the you of today, telling yourself exactly how you were able to get past that impasse. No one will ever have to see your letter but you, so let yourself write freely, not thinking ahead to how you are going to do it, but looking back at how you actually did it, using some wisdom that is inevitably yours but that you might not even know you had.

Another variation on that theme is to imagine yourself advising a good friend on that same problem. You could no doubt help your friend get past the impasse much more easily than you could help yourself. If that's the case, it's because when you're advising someone else, you've taken away the emotional blocks.

All of this illustrates that you have the wisdom within yourself to come through your own transitions and impasses, and that wisdom is something no one can ever take away from you. You can ultimately achieve what you believe you can.

Acting rather than reacting is half the battle. It's been said that when you fail to act, you act to fail, or at the very least, you're relying on luck or other forces you can't control. But once you begin acting as if you have control, you'll never allow yourself to act any other way.

# THIRTEEN

# Ambivalence, Perfectionism, and Procrastination

Are you an ambivalent person? If so, consider this: ambivalence can ruin your life! Ambivalence is the inability to make a decision. Theoretically, if you had everything going for you but were ambivalent about your decision, no matter what you had chosen to do, you could be dwelling on the fact that you should be doing something else. Thus, no matter what kind of life you've made for yourself, ambivalence could ruin it all.

Of course, we all have a certain degree of ambivalence, because life is extremely complex, and things in our lives usually get more complicated as we go along. Actually a certain amount of ambivalence is normal. In fact, a small amount of it might even protect you from being thoughtless about decisions and steps that need to be reasoned out carefully. The problem comes when you allow yourself to operate under the myth that there is one and only one right answer, and if you're indecisive, if you hold out long enough, it'll come to you.

The myth continues with believing that you shouldn't have any regrets about any decisions you do make, so you resist making them at all. But in this case, you might be making decisions by not making any decision at all. By taking no action, you refuse to resolve any problem that contains shades of gray. However, what important issue in life doesn't contain some degree of uncertainty?

Some people simply fear making decisions. If that's you, it's possible that you have many regrets about things that have passed you by, simply because you didn't act decisively when you had the opportunity.

If you think that my statement that ambivalence can ruin your life is a little too strong, then you even may be taking comfort in your ambivalence. My stand on ambivalence is unambivalent: to the extent that it exceeds prudent caution, it will hold you back in any area of your life. This can apply to relationships as well as your career.

When ambivalence discourages you from decision making because of your fear of making a mistake, we call this *perfectionism*. Like ambivalence, perfectionism can be extremely self-defeating. Perfectionism should never be confused with doing your best. It is actually attempting to achieve the impossible. It's demanding that you not make errors, which in essence is a request to be exempted from the rules that define what it is to be human.

Just as ambivalence prevents you from making decisions because of the fear associated with the uncertainty of how those decisions will turn out, perfectionism will stand in the way of decision making through the fear of making a mistake. In addition, perfectionism is one of the main attitudes behind procrastination, which we'll talk about a little later.

Here are some of the beliefs that lie behind perfectionism. See how many of them you can identify with.

- I must do well with at everything I do.
- If I don't set the highest standards for myself, then I'm not really a quality person.
- People will probably think less of me if I make a mistake.
- If I can't excel at something, why attempt it at all?
- If I make a mistake, it's very appropriate that I become upset.
- An average performance is never satisfactory for me.
- One of the worst faults there is is to repeat a mistake.
- Failing is totally unacceptable.
- Those who fail are weak or incompetent.
- I should keep raising my standards and chastising myself for failing to live up to my expectations. Only that degree of self-scrutiny will help me to do better in the future.
- Making an incorrect decision shows you are stupid.

Let me repeat once again the most important point here: when you strive to do your best, that's not being perfectionistic. The negative attitudes of perfectionism are the ones you display towards yourself when, for whatever reason, you miss the mark and put yourself down for it.

Any of the statements above that apply to you need to be reevaluated in order to free you from perfectionism. Perfectionists often feel inadequate because they compare their actual performance with some ideal that doesn't exist, and all of those perfectionistic statements are just that—unrealistic ideals. Giving up perfectionism requires you to look at each of those beliefs and challenge them.

Can you see that perfectionism doesn't equal happiness? Can you possibly meet the standards you impose on yourself? Is trying to meet them worth the cost, and would it be worth the cost even if it were attainable? What is your bottom line for what you are willing to accept as a standard for yourself? If you had heard any of those perfectionistic statements for the first time today, would you believe them? If not, what makes you believe them now?

Procrastination interferes with our decision making as well. You might say that all of us are procrastinators to one extent or another, and whoever coined the term *procrastination* probably counted such positive things as relaxing in that category too. If you were the only person on earth who didn't procrastinate at all, it's awesome to think what you could produce in a lifetime.

Procrastination is the tendency to put off for tomorrow what you could do today, and it's one of the major reasons that people don't accomplish the goals that they set for themselves. Then of course, after you have put something off, you put yourself down for it. Perhaps you spend so much time thinking about your lack of proficiency that you put the task off some more, and then it turns into that familiar vicious cycle.

One day, when I was doing a radio program on procrastination, I asked my listeners what they were most likely to procrastinate on. Overwhelmingly, making decisions seemed to win.

Not all procrastination is bad. After all, there is more to life than completing tasks and making decisions. Sometimes allowing yourself slack and getting away from whatever you're putting off can be quite helpful and refreshing, but that happens when you're doing it consciously, rather than with the ambivalence of having your mind in one place and your actions in another. Sometimes a diversion can help you to see that what you're procrastinating on isn't worthy of attention at all.

When procrastination stifles your long- or short-term objectives, you may want to deal with it as you would any other goal and break it into manageable subgoals. The trick is to make the task less overwhelming so that you can see some light at the end of the tunnel. If you are procrastinating on making a decision, look for the perfectionistic thinking that makes you fear an unfavorable outcome of that decision. The great decision makers in history, such as Harry Truman, understood that the consequences of not deciding were usually worse than those of making a decision that in hindsight you would second-guess.

What decisions are you contemplating? If you've read this book up to this point, no doubt there are many aspects of your life that you've reexamined. With the attitudes you've acquired or at least tried, perhaps you made some new decisions.

Now I would like you to think about some decisions that still need to be made. Try looking at some issue in your life without the obstacles of ambivalence or perfectionism. To do that, try this *hedonic calculus* exercise.

The word *hedonic* refers to a process that when done, will give you pleasure, but the type of hedonism we're striving for in this exercise is long-term hedonism, that's consistent with the goals you have set.

On a piece of paper, write the options that you're considering regarding a decision you would like to make. List all the pros and cons of each option, assigning a score from one to ten next to each pro or con. Next, add up your score for all of the things going *for* each of the possible outcomes of your decision and the score for each of the things going *against* it. Add up your score and get your total for pros and cons.

Next, take one more step—and this is what actually makes it an exercise in hedonism. Step back and ask yourself what aspect of the decision will in the long run (and that can be whatever you define it to be) serve you the most, that is, will give you the most amount of pleasure.

Is it the outcome that came out numerically, or is it a different one? The important thing is that you have the power to override a logical solution to the problem (which is usually what will come out numerically) by looking at what you feel is in your long-term best interest.

If the two answers conflict, still make a choice. Yes, it's OK to go with the nonnumerical one. The important thing is to make a choice, stick to it, and stand behind it, even if it later turns out that you should have done something differently.

If you're finding this to be difficult, look at your underlying attitude. What's holding you back? Is it your fear of making the wrong decision? Are you looking for certainty where certainty does not exist? Are you insisting that no decision can be made as long as there is any ambivalence? Can you find another fear or obstacle that's holding you back?

The golden rule for making decisions is that all decisions are, in reality, made on the basis of incomplete data. If you knew the outcome, then you certainly wouldn't be struggling to make a decision at all, would you? If you're insisting that that be the case before you make the decision, you now know exactly why you are as decision averse as you may be!

The strategies in this book will help you to gain mastery over the attitudes that govern much of your life. Sometimes repetition is what's needed to master the particular difficult areas you choose to work on. But it's well worth it, as the rewards for taking charge of each and every aspect of your life are infinite!

# FOURTEEN

# Questions and Answers

## Man

*In the last year and a half, I've been through three jobs. How can I possibly maintain a positive attitude when everything always seems to go wrong?*

## Dr. Broder

First of all, let's talk about how you say everything always seems to go wrong. That particular mind-set, more than anything else, is going to defeat you, because you start to predict that the next thing's going to go wrong also.

I think the first step is to take a look at each of the three jobs, see why each one panned out the way it did, and see the different variables. Maybe there are certain things you need to do differently. On the other hand, maybe there are certain things that were not quite your fault. I think you have to look at all the different factors here and start doing a little bit of problem solving. The most important thing is not to put yourself down for it, because all that does is reduce the confidence you have in yourself to do well on the next job.

## Woman

*Why can't I seem to let myself get involved again since my last relationship broke up?*

## Dr. Broder

It's very possible that you're telling yourself that, should you get involved again and this relationship, like the last one, didn't work out, you would totally be unable to handle it. One not so great way to protect yourself from that kind of hurt in the future is to not let yourself get involved.

Ask yourself, "What would be so terrible if I were to get involved, and the relationship again didn't turn out to be the one that lasts?" If you can accept that as a possibility— not as something you would choose, but as a possibility— and allow yourself to make another wrong choice, then you won't have the fear of getting involved again.

Meeting people is nothing more than a set of attitudes. When you're ready, the right person will come along. I've shown that to people time and time again throughout the years, and there's no reason it shouldn't work for you either.

## Man

*If someone's done me wrong, why shouldn't I be angry at them?*

## Dr. Broder

Because it's not to your advantage to be angry. See, anger is painful to you. Think about how you feel when you're feeling angry. Is it the other person who's suffering, or is it you? Once you realize how self-destructive that emotion is and how much it's to your own selfish advantage to let go of it, you'll certainly do your best to spare yourself that pain.

When someone has done you wrong, once again, if you can get beyond that emotional screen called anger, you can look at the situation and problem-solve. That might mean dealing with that person differently, avoiding that person altogether, or maybe accepting the fact that certain people are going to do you wrong, and that's part of being a member of the human race.

## Woman

*I try to take risks, but then I usually end up falling back on my old, comfortable ways. How can I be more daring?*

## Dr. Broder

First, you need to realize that what you perceive as the result of taking your risk—and that could be some kind of catastrophe—rarely will occur. That's the key. Sometimes we avoid taking risks because we get into a rut or a comfortable state of discomfort. If you can see that it's to your advantage to make yourself just a little bit uncomfortable temporarily, you'll find that you can become friends with that discomfort. Then it won't be so intimidating. But if you're waiting for it not to have any level of discomfort, then you have a long wait.

People who want that never learn to take risks. It's just like when you learned how to swim: there was a second when you had to go underwater, and that was before you knew you could get out. Then you learned how to swim. Just about every risk that you'll take throughout your life will be like that to some degree.

## Woman

*Why is it I always feel guilty when I have to say no to someone, and what can I do to stop that guilt?*

## Dr. Broder

When you're saying no to someone, all you're really doing is expressing your own preference. Just as someone is asking you to do something that you would say no to, and they're expressing their preference, you have the same right. So your guilt is really an irrational feeling. Sometimes it's because you imagine that if you say no to someone, they're not going to like you, and if somebody doesn't like you, that'll be a terrible situation.

Saying no, like doing anything else, gets easier each time you do it, and once you've learned to assert yourself, you won't have it any other way. So consider the first time you say no to be a risk. Even if you have a little bit of guilt, it's not going to kill you, although it might be a little uncomfortable. As long as you know that that guilt is not based on the fact that you did something wrong but on part of you telling yourself, "I should please others even more than myself," then little by little you'll learn to feel it less. Eventually you will know in your gut that you have as much of a right to self-determination as anyone else.

## Man

*I've just gotten divorced after sixteen years of marriage. All I think about is the way it used to be. What can I do to let go of these feelings?*

## Dr. Broder

When you think of the way it used to be, are you thinking about the circumstances that led to the breakup? Are you thinking about the issues that you had? Very few people who go through a divorce don't go through a period of time when they're feeling extremely overwhelmed by the issues that are going on with their partner.

If you're looking back and just remembering the good times, then you're not looking at the whole picture. Maybe you need to talk to people you were in touch with at the time of the breakup; maybe they can remind you of some of the things that you went through.

Sometimes, too, we get addicted not only to a person, but to a lifestyle. It could be not so much that you miss the other person, but you miss the lifestyle of being part of a couple. You'll have that again when you get reinvolved, but you probably won't get reinvolved until you can let go of the old relationship.

## Woman

*I'm trying to get over the death of a loved one, and I'm having a hard time. Since it happened six months ago, I've been really depressed. Is this normal, or could a different attitude help me?*

## Dr. Broder

Getting over the death of a loved one involves grieving and getting rid of a lot of feelings of acute sadness and loneliness. Sometimes there's even some guilt in there, about things that you may not have said to the person that you wanted to say. Sometimes there's anger. It's a very complex array of emotions, and everyone grieves in his or her own way.

So you need to give yourself permission to grieve. The key word here is *permission*. If you can give yourself permission to have all these feelings, and you see them starting to lessen over a period of time, then you know you're healing.

If not, you may want to join a support group of others who are going through the grieving process. You may also want to spend some time around other people who may be missing this individual as well, and give yourselves some support.

After six months, it's still very appropriate to be grieving. If you're still in that process after a year, I would consider getting some professional help.

## Woman

*As an incest survivor, I've had a great deal of difficulty throughout my life trusting men. Is there a positive attitude that can help turn this around?*

## Dr. Broder

What you're doing is taking an extremely unfortunate situation and not allowing yourself to heal by overgeneralizing: because there was a man in your life early on that you couldn't trust, who took dreadfully unfair advantage of you, all men are going to be the same way.

This is an overgeneralization error; once you recognize it, you can work on it. There are many, many decent men who will be very nourishing toward you and who don't have to trigger those emotions.

The first step is to believe that there is an alternative. I would also suggest that you join a support group for incest survivors, especially one that is led by somebody who has satisfactorily been able to let go of this part of her past. You need to see that it can be done, and you need support in letting yourself heal. Then you'll be able to have as good a relationship as anyone else, regardless of your background.

## Man

*My job requires me to meet serious deadlines. How can I control the constant stress I'm always feeling?*

## Dr. Broder

One key is planning, and that is a logistical thing. You need to allow a little bit of Murphy's Law to kick in: new things will practically always come up that will tax you, challenge you, take up your time. If you make your schedule too tight, then there are things that are going to make you overtax your system, because there's only so much a person can do.

The attitudinal part of this is to realize that you suffer from the same human frailties as everyone else. You can't do it all, you do have limitations, and it's to your advantage not to overburden yourself so that it takes away from your quality of life. It's your quality of life that should be in the forefront.

What is this job for? What's the purpose of it? The purpose of it is, either directly or indirectly, to bring you some happiness, but if that happiness is being wrecked by your not being able to enjoy the pleasures that are associated with your job, then you're missing out on a great deal.

## Woman

*I guess you could say I've had poor self-esteem since I was a child. My parents always made me feel like I couldn't do anything right. How can I change this?*

## Dr. Broder

How you were as a child and how you are today have one very important difference, and that is the fact that you are now able to use a very well-developed adult mind to determine what is appropriate and what isn't appropriate. You didn't have that advantage when you were a child.

Ask yourself this: if you heard that you were inadequate for the first time today, would you believe it? Of course you wouldn't. You wouldn't believe it if you heard it for the first time today, but when you continue to believe it, you act as though it were valid information.

When we're children, we're gullible, and we believe things that people tell us; often we believe that we have no choice. Very often as children, we *don't* have choices. As an adult, you have a choice, and the one choice that no one can ever take away from you is how you feel about yourself. This is the time to give that feeling up. Your life will turn around immeasurably.

## Man

*All my life I've lived day-to-day. I'm happy, but I just don't seem to be accomplishing as much as I wanted to. How can I become a goal-oriented person?*

## Dr. Broder

Being a goal-oriented person is a matter of learning certain habits. Look ahead at what you would like to accomplish. Make an ironclad commitment to yourself that you're going to stay within the parameters that you've chosen. That's sometimes easier said than done, especially if you've not done it before, but becoming a goal-oriented person will only happen when you see how goals work for you, how they make your life a lot less stressful, and how they give you more accomplishments that are important to you.

As you develop that ability and it becomes second nature to you, you won't operate any other way. The first thing to do is to start with some very simple goals, and build on them. Let yourself have some small successes. When you see the difference in what you can accomplish by using some of these goal-setting methods, then try something a little bit more difficult. Try to get a little bit more under that goal umbrella. Eventually you will plan everything that way, because not only will it be a lot more efficient, but you'll be a lot more satisfied with the end result.

# Man

*I'm a recovering alcoholic. When I've slipped and given into my cravings, I've really hated myself. In fact, it's this self-hatred that often keeps me from slipping again. Do you still say to give up all sources of self-hatred?*

# Dr. Broder

Oh, yes, because self-hatred is probably a lot of the reason that you drink in the first place. Drinking and drugs anesthetize you to self-hatred. Sometimes when you feel the pain of not accepting the person you are, the anesthesia of drugs or alcohol temporarily feels very good. The behavior can be very loathsome. It's fine to loathe the behavior of drinking.

Should you slip again, it's fine to consider your goal of abstinence as not being met, but it is not at all to your advantage to make you stop accepting yourself, because it's only a part of you that is responsible for the drinking behavior. The part of you that's asking the question, of course, is healthy. The part of you that's asking the question knows that drinking is not to your best interest. Acknowledge that part of you too.

# Man

*I've been involved in a court case that's been dragging on for over two years now. No matter how hard I try, I'm always feeling frustrated. What can I do?*

# Dr. Broder

It sounds like you're worrying about something that you can't change right now. In life, there are lots of things like that, things that aren't able to be resolved when you want to resolve them.

I think the first step is to do whatever you can do to solve the problem, and then learn to let go of it. When you get a thought that is not to your advantage, you might want to use some of the methods of thought stopping. They will help you stop thinking about something that is either an obsession or is so repetitious that your thought process just isn't helping you to understand, accept, or solve the problem.

Some people can just use a thought-stopping technique by saying, "There it goes again," and say, "Stop," or they can divert themselves, say, by listening to music. One of my favorite techniques is the rubber-band approach I mentioned earlier.

Very often something that keeps coming up in your mind is going to force you to address it at that level, but you can't decide consciously that you're not going to think about something. If I were to tell you right now not to think about telephone poles, the first thing you'd do is think about a telephone pole. So remember: your thoughts are not always under your control, but we can use some methods to shape them. The first step is to realize you're dealing with an unwanted thought, and for all intents and purposes, that's what this court case is.

## Woman

*I'm a single woman, and I'm having a very hard time meeting men who are interested in a committed relationship. Is there any way my attitude can help me here?*

## Dr. Broder

My experience over the years has been that when you are ready and when your attitude is right, the right person will come along. The first step is to meet a lot of people, and many people don't like that idea.

There are really two attitudes that go with meeting potential relationships. The one is what I call the *Schwab's drugstore approach*. Schwab's drugstore was the place where Lana Turner was supposedly discovered by sipping a soda and got her first job as a movie star. (By the way, that's not correct, but it's a great story.) Lots of people sit and just wait for the right person to come along or try to make everyone that comes along the right person.

I have found that that's not the winning attitude when it comes to finding a good relationship. The winning attitude is one where you recognize that it's a numbers game. Whether you like it or not, it's a numbers game. You need to meet a lot of people. Over the course of time, you'll meet some people who will be attracted to you that you won't find the least bit attractive. You'll meet people you are attracted to who won't be attracted to you. You'll meet some people where you'll be like two ships passing in the night: there won't be any attraction at all. You might meet some people that you'll be friends with, but there won't be enough chemistry to really have a romance. Eventually you'll meet one person with whom you'll have enough commonality so that the two of you will be able to get something going.

You have to take the responsibility to meet numbers of people. This could be through personal ads. It could be through going to different events. It could be through going to singles vacations or taking fun courses.

There's an infinite number of ways to meet people, but you need to realize that the more particular you are about the person you wind up with, the more difficult it's going to be to meet that person. But if you can accept the fact that it's going to involve meeting a lot of people, eventually, like everyone else, you'll find the right person, I assure you.

## Man

*Every time I start to make a change in my life, something inside me says, "Don't do it. Play it safe." Will I ever be able to make a change for the better?*

## Dr. Broder

You sure will, as soon as you tell that voice to leave you alone and let you lead your life. That's your voice, and there's no rule of the universe that says you have to listen to it. Remember, you're in charge. Perhaps it's an old tape that you've been listening to your entire life, but it is never too late to change.

I've seen people make significant life changes in their seventies and eighties, and I've seen people learn to take their life in their hands at a very young age. The key is that as soon as you decide that you're going to do it, that voice doesn't have to control you anymore.

## Woman

*Whenever I get into social situations, I usually feel physically anxious. How can I help myself to overcome this?*

## Dr. Broder

Feeling physically anxious is not so bad a thing. If you stop and think about it, it's the fact that you recoil from that feeling to the point where you'll do anything to avoid it that's probably more painful than the feeling itself.

The next time, try to do whatever you would do whether you had that feeling or not, and see what difference it makes. See how quickly that anxiety dissipates. In other words, act as if you're able to conquer that anxiety, and you'll conquer it for sure.

## Man

*Ever since my wife and I made up our minds that we were going to have a child, I've had sexual difficulties. Could my attitude be causing this problem?*

## Dr. Broder

You may want to look at your attitude about whether having a child is something that you want to do, whether you're ambivalent about it, whether there are some fears associated with it. For some people, the fears could be financial. They could be fears of getting less attention from your wife. There could be all kinds of worries regarding your new lifestyle once the baby is born, and of course, one way to avoid dealing with all that is not to have a baby; by becoming impotent, that will be assured.

I would suggest that you really look at your feelings about having a child at this time in your life. Are you doing it because you want to, or are you doing it because for some reason you have to, or because you're giving in?

## Woman

*My child was killed by a drunk driver. How can I ever be positive about anything again?*

## Dr. Broder

I don't think that there's a circumstance that any of us could possibly face that could come close to the magnitude of the grief that would accompany the death of a child, especially something like that. Let's face it. We expect our children to bury us, not the other way around.

However, the grief, as intense and as real as it is, can be worked through over a period of time. My strong suggestion to you would be that you join a support group for grieving parents. There are many of them around the country. I know that they're in all the big cities. Parents who have lost children can commiserate with each other, and, somehow over a period of time, purge this grief out of their system.

Nothing can bring your child back. Even if you could, you know that your child wouldn't want you to feel the pain you're feeling, nor would you want anyone to feel that kind of pain about you. You would want them to move on with their lives as best they can. You'll never erase this completely, nor would you probably want to, but you certainly can get on with your life. The first and most important thing is for you to acknowledge that this is possible, and then get the support you need.

## Woman

*Will there be a point when I don't have to listen to inspirational tapes or read inspirational books anymore, and it will become sort of automatic, or will I have to keep reminding myself of these principles throughout my whole life?*

## Dr. Broder

All of us have something that we have more trouble dealing with than someone else may have. When you come up against those obstacles, you may want to turn to the appropriate inspirational tape or book for a little reinforcement. Whether you'll need it for your entire life, of course, is up to you.

How well you've integrated the material and how much you need to change certain attitudes is a highly individual matter, but I would suggest that you don't make a demand on yourself that you be this finished product that is beyond any form of growth. Once you've done that, then you're opening yourself up for new life circumstances that come along to test you in ways you haven't been tested before.

You may want to put inspirational books and tapes aside for a while, but don't be so perfectionistic that you put demands on yourself that you not need a little reinforcement now and then. I think that to some degree, we all do.

## Man

*Whenever I get in a bind, I just seem to put things off until they go away. How can I learn to take action?*

## Dr. Broder

If you know that you procrastinate, then you know what you need to do to stop. The question is, can you use the willpower to push yourself in the right direction? That's the key to getting out of procrastination.

The next thing is to set goals, break them down into chunks that you can manage, and get some support in carrying them out. Sometimes people can work through procrastination in pairs. You might have a friend who has a project that he or she is procrastinating on who can act as not only a support, but also a prodder for you, and you can reciprocate. That can start the ball rolling.

You need to determine why it's to your advantage to stop procrastinating, and then look at the benefits to yourself in doing so. Once you can do that, you're on the road.

## Man

*I have a history of panic attacks. Can I use positive attitude training to control my tendency to panic?*

## Dr. Broder

Panic attacks have two components. One is physiological, and the other is behavioral. Some people who get panic attacks need to be medicated, or at least evaluated medically in order to bring the attacks under control.

If, however, we assume that the medical part is under control, the next step in dealing with your panic attack is to think through just what is the fear if you temporarily get yourself into a situation where you're suffering from some loss of control. Panic attacks are usually the fear of loss of control.

Sometimes using the exercise called the emotional fire drill will help you to rehearse that situation and to come up with alternatives. People who are prone to panic attacks can find it helpful to make a list of things that they can do when a panic attack starts. This very often averts the attack. Having a plan that you can fall back on is the key here.

## FIFTEEN

# Positive-Attitude Booster and Summary

This chapter is what I call a positive-attitude booster that will summarize much of what was said throughout this book. You can turn to it whenever you need a booster shot or a quick reminder that your attitudes and well-being are almost completely within your control.

Sometimes in the routine of everyday life, that perspective can be forgotten, but by turning to this chapter when you need it or rereading it approximately once a month, these ideas for acquiring your crucial positive attitudes will become more and more a hardwired part of you.

Remember, if you believe that the way you feel inside is determined only by events outside of yourself, then unless you're a very lucky person, very often you're going to feel out of control and powerless, and as though you've been dealt a dirty deal. But it's your attitudes that predispose you to the way you feel, think, or behave. You can not only learn but continue to develop the positive attitudes that will give you mastery over practically any life situation, beginning with how you feel about yourself, the other people around you, and the world in general.

Anytime you get hung up on a particular area, go back to the chapter that deals with that specific issue to develop the winning attitude you need the most.

Remember that your life is a process for which you are ultimately responsible. This includes not only your behavior but the way you feel about things as well. Behind practically every negative attitude, there's a *should* statement that we make, consciously or unconsciously, that leads to that disturbing emotion.

For example, if you're feeling angry, ask yourself what expectations you're demanding should be better met, or how you are telling yourself that someone should have treated you better. If you're feeling depressed, look at how you may be down on yourself by demanding that you should perform better than your best, or how you may be thinking that life is terrible and catastrophic when it doesn't go the way you want it to.

If you're feeling dissatisfied, are you being perfectionistic, or is there a problem to be addressed? Have you labeled yourself in a globally negative way simply because you've made a mistake or failed in a task rather than recognizing that, if anything, it's merely the act that deserves a negative label?

Are you confusing insight with hindsight? Insight occurs when you learn a valuable life lesson. Hindsight, on the other hand, is telling yourself that you should have done something differently at a time when you were not privy to all the information that you have now. Again, you can have practically anything you want in life, but you probably can't have everything you want, no matter how hard you try. Therefore it's essential that you accept this limitation, which all of us have in common.

If your goal is achieving peace of mind, peace of mind can be defined as those moments that are free of shoulds. Peace of mind is achieved when you're not telling yourself you should do better, someone else should treat you better, or the world should be easy, or one of the many infinite variations of those themes.

If you've noticed yourself getting upset lately, you may want to start keeping a log of your thoughts. What triggers those negative thoughts, and what attitude needs to be zeroed in on? Is it your low frustration tolerance, LFT? Is there something that you're telling yourself is too hard when it's merely difficult, or something you are allowing yourself to believe that you can't stand? LFT is really discomfort anxiety. To the extent that you let yourself believe that you can't stand discomfort, you'll avoid all kinds of situations that could be beneficial to you.

If this is going on, imagine someone you cared about who's bothered by the very thing that is triggering your LFT. How would you advise that person? Chances are, you would give them lots of support in standing the thing they're telling themselves they can't stand.

People will treat you the way they choose to treat you. Hopefully, this will be positive and pleasant, but sometimes it won't. Get rid of all those illusions that you can control other people, the world, or certain events in it, because you can't. On the other hand, no one can really hurt you emotionally unless you allow it.

The next time you get angry, instead of blaming the anger on the other person, attribute your anger to your own attitude about that other person. Then you're fully in control again.

The same holds true for other emotions, such as depression and anxiety. Depression is often a feeling of hopelessness—being stuck in a situation that you tell yourself you would not choose and one that you believe you cannot change. Sometimes depression is merely anger turned inward at your own inability to change things that are out of your control. What can be more self-defeating than that?

If you recognize yourself in that situation, let go of it. Self-blame will only defeat you. If you define yourself as incompetent, then you've turned your attitude into a vicious circle. Not only have you put yourself down, but you may have undermined your own ability to change things in the future that very well may be under your control.

Know what is within your power to change and what isn't. Those things that aren't within your power to change need only be accepted. This involves releasing yourself from that self-imposed burden to change what in fact cannot be changed. The instant you see something as being out of your power to change, walk away from it. You may short-cut that depression right on the spot.

As far as anxiety, fear of the unknown, is concerned, remember it's really the feeling of fear, but with a twist. You are pretending a situation has dire consequences when it really does not. Fear of ridicule or criticism, fear of rejection, fear of failure, fear of change, and sometimes even the fear of fear itself are all forms of anxiety. Perhaps the most common is performance anxiety. A little bit of performance anxiety can actually improve your performance in such things as exams and presentations. But underneath it is the attitude that you will be the subject of unspeakable ridicule if you fail, or that you yourself could never accept less than an optimal performance.

There comes a point where performance anxiety becomes a self-fulfilling prophecy, when it begins to affect your performance negatively. You can allow this to happen by catastrophizing: imagining and fearing that the worst possible thing will occur and that you won't be able to handle it.

To confront performance anxiety, do some breathing, relaxing more with each breath out, and imagine your anxiety becoming excitement. Remember, anxiety and excitement are physiologically identical. It's only the negative label that makes it anxiety rather than excitement.

A mental expression of anxiety is worry. It often comes in the form of unwanted thoughts. Often, they will burn out on their own power if you don't reinforce them by acting as though they contain messages you need to hear. Here it's important to see the difference between those things that you have the power to affect and those things that you don't. When you define something as out of your power, worry becomes even more pointless.

Bringing your negative emotions under control is a function of changing the belief that causes them. You can try this simple imagery exercise to bring practically any emotion under control.

Close your eyes and imagine a situation in which you would typically feel anxious. Imagine the thing you are most anxious about actually occurring. Imagine the results being just what you most feared they would be. Be aware of how awful you're telling yourself that fear is, and notice how the feeling of anxiety increases.

With your eyes still closed, relabel that feeling of anxiety as excitement, and reframe the struggle as challenge. Ask yourself, "What's the worst possible thing that could happen if I really flub this? I'll look ridiculous. I won't succeed this time." See how taking away the element of catastrophe lessens the anxiety.

Anxiety is one of the emotions that we connect the most to distress. Distress is the amount of stress that we have over and above that which we are managing or coping with. Stressors themselves are simply the pressures of daily living, but the culprit is distress.

One of the main causes of stress is changes. These can occur in a work or home situation. More typically, we tend to put numerous stressors on ourselves. Perhaps by over-planning our days and engaging in too many activities, we don't allow ourselves to relax.

Hurry sickness not only causes us to have excess amounts of stress, but also tends to dilute the enjoyment of life. Having impossible goals and impossible deadlines all contribute. Symptoms of stress can be emotional as well as physical, and stress sometimes can even become circular. For example, if you're under a lot of stress, you could be neglecting your most important relationships, and that could cause you more stress by inadvertently abusing some of your most important sources of support.

So keep your goals realistic, and allow yourself to experience some satisfaction with what you have before pressing yourself more for what you don't have. Let yourself enjoy the fruits of your hard-earned labor rather than negating the progress you've made simply by reaching for more, perhaps unattainable, goals.

Keep long-term versus short-term consequences in the forefront when taking on new things.

It may help you to keep a diary of stressful situations, including negative feelings that come up for you. Try to be as specific as you can about exactly what it is that's triggering stress in you. Look for new alternatives, especially when you are between the occurrences of stressors. You know your attitudes are changing when you can look back on your diary later and see that the same things that were so difficult for you at one time now don't have nearly the same impact.

Make a list of all the things you feel good about and that make you feel good. When you're under the gun, take a look at that list so you can find some positive things to support you.

Hobbies such as sports, sailing, or other relaxing activities can provide a great diversion when you're feeling distress. If you don't have the time to leave what you're doing and actually do something positive, then take a mental break, and imagine yourself doing something very relaxing. Even two or three minutes of this can make all the difference in the world when stressors are piling up on you.

Also, return to the simple relaxation exercise that I gave at the end of Chapter Six. Some people learn how to do this quite easily. With others, it takes some effort, but I've had people tell me that a twenty-minute experience with this exercise can feel as relaxing as a two-week vacation. Never consider taking time out to relax as a waste of time. It will infinitely increase your ability to manage your stressors, and that can add hours to your day.

You can use the relaxation exercise or any part of it to help you to do just about any visualization. Throughout this book, I've given many such exercises. Visualizing helps us to see our potential perhaps more clearly than we could in any other way. We can visualize having a positive self-image during those times when we're down. We can use visualization to imagine having a rewarding attitude during a period of time when we feel trapped with a self-defeating one. We can use visualization to imagine taking a risk and having it come out the worst possible way, or having it come out the best possible way. Having a preview of the potential on both sides, we can make better choices.

Visualization can provide some very important help in setting goals and imagining certain changes that could otherwise seem intimidating.

Are you procrastinating on something? Well, in addition to attacking your attitude, try visualizing that thing you're procrastinating on as being finished. Then, when you set out to break down the task into manageable parts, see how much easier the task appears.

Finally, you can use visualization to dream. Close your eyes and take a few minutes to get yourself into a state of relaxation. Imagine yourself being totally happy by whatever definition of happiness you've made for yourself. Imagine you're able to form good social relationships, whether they be romantic ones or just friendships. Imagine that you're exactly as connected or detached as you want to be.

Imagine that your work is as creative and productive as you want it to be. Imagine that it has great meaning for you and that you are able to perform well when things get tough by selecting the attitude that will work for you and not allowing yourself to get pulled in any negative directions.

Imagine yourself really accepting the person you are. Imagine a self-image that's positive, so that when you look into a mirror, you really like the person you see, being in a frame of mind where there are no shoulds, no demands that you're making on yourself or anyone else, where you're able to savor the benefits that you've worked so hard for.

Everything that I've asked you to imagine is within your own power, not only to imagine, but to enjoy right now. They're all a function of the attitudes by which you are capable of choosing to live your life. Take a few moments to savor and enjoy that feeling, knowing that you can always return to this place within yourself any time you choose. When you are ready, slowly open your eyes.

The way you live your live is nothing more than the sum total of the choices you make for yourself. I hope that by using the ideas in this book, you will consistently choose the attitude that will make your life work better and better the more you apply them. Personal growth, like life itself, is an ongoing process. Give it the attention it needs, and it will work wonders for you.

Good luck, and remember: don't take yourself too seriously.

# About the Author

Michael S. Broder, Ph.D., is a psychologist, best-selling author, speaker, media personality, and coach to high achievers. His work centers around helping people to bring about major change in the shortest time possible.

An acclaimed expert in cognitive-behavioral therapy, Dr. Broder lives and practices in Philadelphia, PA. For over forty years, he has treated thousands of individuals and couples, including some of our highest achievers in business, politics, sports, and the media.

Michael is the author of many popular books—including *Seven Steps to Your Best Life: The Stage Climbing Solution for Living the Life You Were Born to Live, The Art of Living Single, Secrets of Sexual Ecstasy,* and *Can Your Relationship Be Saved?*—as well as scores of highly acclaimed self-help audio programs.

For many years, he hosted the radio program *Psychologically Speaking With Dr. Michael Broder.* Michael has made guest appearances on the *Today* Show, *Oprah*, and over a thousand other TV and radio programs; has been written about in *TIME*, *Newsweek*, *USA Today*, *The New York Times*, *The Wall Street Journal,* and hundreds of other top publications.

Dr. Broder earned his Ph.D. at Temple University. He conducts seminars, talks, and presentations to professional as well as lay audiences worldwide; he has trained many thousands of psychologists, psychiatrists, clinical social workers, and other mental health professionals.

Michael Broder can be emailed directly MB@MichaelBroder.com. Or visit DrMichaelBroder.com where you can obtain complimentary downloads for audio programs and workbooks that will give you additional help for such things as anxiety, depression, anger, transitioning through life changes, stress management, self-confidence, and a wide variety of relationship issues.